77 Powerful Methods To Get More Kindle eBook Sales

Marc Guberti

How Would Your Life Change If Your Kindle eBooks Made $100,000 Annually?

It is easier than ever to get your books published. There are millions of self-published authors who publish their eBooks on Kindle, and based on where we are heading, that number will continue to rise. Although there are numerous self-published authors and eBooks on Kindle, few people are able to earn a full-time income from their Kindle eBooks. According to a survey from *Digital Book World And Writer's Digest*, self-published authors do not make a lot of money from their Kindle eBooks. The median income range for self-published authors is under $5,000 every year. In addition, only 1.8% of self-published authors make over $100,000 annually from their Kindle eBooks.

Although the statistics look bleak, there is a reason why not as many self-published authors are able to earn full-time incomes from their Kindle eBooks. The reason this problem exists is that few self-published authors know the right methods to use to get more sales and build an audience. Many self-published authors go to Amazon with the hopes that Amazon will do all of the work for them. These self-published authors think that since Amazon gets millions of unique visitors every day, one of those visitors will surely see and buy your Kindle eBook. In the beginning of your self-publishing career, Amazon will not promote your Kindle eBook right away, and when many self-published authors realize it requires a lot of work to make a full-time income from their Kindle eBooks, these self-published authors have no sense of direction. Since they thought it would be easy, these self-published authors do not know the course of action they need to take in order to increase their sales. A majority of self-published authors do not know how to make more connections with other people and convert them into customers. This is why self-published authors are not able to make sales. It's not because self-publishing is dead. It is only because no one is explaining the methods self-published authors need to implement to generate more sales.

It is very possible to become a successful self-published author. The 1.8% proves that it is possible for any self-published author to make over $100,000 annually for their Kindle eBooks. There is potential. In addition, the 1.8% gives self-published authors the hope they need to continue writing Kindle eBooks. Self-published authors see the results, and some self-published authors believe they can eventually get those results as well.

Now let's go back to the question. How would your life change if you were making $100,000 every year by selling your own Kindle eBooks? Would you be able to quit your job, go on more vacations, have more money to pay for your child's college, get rid of your debt, or do something else with that $100,000 every year? There are numerous ways that your life can change if your Kindle eBooks generated $100,000 in sales every year. If you are like most people, your Kindle eBooks are not making $100,000 every year. You may be making thousands of dollars every year, or a little over $10,000 every year if you're lucky. No matter what you write about, it is possible to make $100,000 every year by selling your Kindle eBooks.

In order for your Kindle eBooks to make $100,000 annually, you need a course of action. In this book, I am going to provide you with 77 different methods that I use to get more sales for my Kindle eBooks. In addition, I will provide you with a course of action that you need to take with these methods. In other books about boosting your sales, readers are given the methods but have to guess on what direction they need to take. Instead of taking the typical approach, this book will show you exactly how to implement these methods so you can see your Kindle eBook sales rise exponentially.

Here are the contents of this book:

Methods 1-12: Growing A Powerful Presence On The Web

In order to become a successful self-published author, you need to grow a powerful presence for yourself on the web so potential customers know that your Kindle eBooks exist and become buyers. The people won't come just because you published your own Kindle eBook. If you grow a powerful presence on the web and promote your Kindle eBooks, then the people will come. Getting on Amazon does not mean you are automatically going to get hundreds of sales every day. In order to go from zero sales every day to hundreds of sales every day, you need to build an audience of people who are eager to buy your next Kindle eBook before it comes out.

Method #1: Create A Blog

Creating a blog is an essential way to get more Kindle eBook sales. On your blog, you have the power to grab people's attention and lead them to your Kindle eBooks. You can promote your Kindle eBooks on your blog's sidebar (the pictures that appear to the left or right of your blog's content) and separate pages on your blog. Promoting your Kindle eBooks on your blog will get the customer's undivided attention before any other Kindle eBook on Amazon can steal that attention. One of the reasons why some people do not buy your Kindle eBooks is because they see another Kindle eBook in the "Customers Also Bought" section that they would prefer to have. No matter how many times you call Amazon, they will not take down the "Customers Also Bought" option for your Kindle eBook sales pages. Getting someone to see your Kindle eBook on your blog will entice that person to purchase your Kindle eBook before looking at Amazon's "Customers Also Bought" section.

Before your visitor goes on Amazon, that visitor needs to be absolutely convinced that your Kindle eBook is the right one for them. If your potential customer is uncertain about whether your eBook is the right one, that potential customer will start to explore other options. Once the potential customer starts to explore other options, then you may be lose the sale. Having a blog to promote your Kindle eBooks gives you an advantage to highlight your own Kindle eBooks.

The main point of having a blog is to get your visitors to focus on your eBooks while providing free content such as daily blog posts and the occasional video. Many visitors believe (rightfully so) that the content on a blog reflects the content in a Kindle eBook. If your blog contains quality content, then your visitors will believe that your Kindle eBooks contain quality content as well.

How Frequently Should You Update Your Blog?
In order to become a successful writer, you must write new content every day. Writing new content allows you to improve as a writer and be more comfortable with writing longer, quality info-packed Kindle eBooks. You should be able to publish 1 blog post every day of the week. By publishing one blog post every day, you will be obligated to write content every day and be less likely to give up as a self-published author.

The more frequently you publish blog posts the more times your readers get to get familiar with your content and writing. This is a powerful way to build trust with your readers. What many people do not know is that trust comes from being seen frequently. The reason you trust a best friend more than an acquaintance is because you see that best friend more often than you see the other friend. As you consistently write one blog post every day over a long period of time, your readers will see you more often. If they read enough of your blog posts, they are more likely to buy your Kindle eBooks due to familiarity.

How Long Should Your Blog Posts Be?

The typical blog post should be between 250-1,000 words. However, if you go slightly under 250 words or slightly above 1,000 words, that is okay. Some of my blog posts go under 250 words when I only need a few sentences to convey a message. These types of short blog posts are rare. Some of my blog posts are longer than 1,000 words because I wanted to go in depth about a certain topic. If you are writing several thousand words every day for your Kindle eBooks, then fitting in 250-1,000 words every day for a blog post will be easy to implement. While you are looking at the word count, it is also important to provide quality content for your readers. Do not be redundant and wordy just to get more words in your blog posts or your Kindle eBooks.

Method #2: Make It Easy For People To See Your Product On Your Blog

There will be people who go on your blog who will want to buy your Kindle eBooks. However, the only way these people can buy your Kindle eBooks is if they see those Kindle eBooks. Your customer can't buy what he can't see. If you were looking for a book in a big bookstore, you would be less likely to find that book if it was all the way in the back of the bookstore. If the book you wanted was in the front of the bookstore, you would be more likely to find it (and buy it).

When you have a picture of your book on your blog, that picture needs to be large enough to get noticed. A 50 by 50 pixel picture does not get noticed as much as a 200 by 400 pixel picture. In addition, if you write really long blog posts, your readers will see a blank white space at your sidebar when they scroll down to the bottom of your blog post. The problem this creates is that once the person likes your blog posts and is thinking about buying your Kindle eBook, they only see a white space. It is entirely possible that the potential customer scrolls up to see your Kindle eBook again. However, you will be more likely to make the sale if the customer always sees your Kindle eBook at the side of your blog post. The solution is to have the images of your Kindle eBooks be fixed widgets on your blog. That way, when someone scrolls down, your Kindle eBook's image scrolls down too. When your potential customers are done reading your blog post, they see your Kindle eBook. Even if a potential customer does not buy your Kindle eBook the first time, that customer may eventually buy one of your Kindle eBooks if they consistently visit your blog and continue to read your content.

Make Sure People Can Read The Title And Subtitle

When you promote a Kindle eBook on your blog, the cover is very important. When you size your Kindle eBook's image, your potential customers must be able to read the title and subtitle. If words in your title and subtitle are blurry when you add your Kindle eBook's image to your sidebar, reshape the image until it is easy for anyone to read the words in your Kindle eBook's title and subtitle.

Add A Caption To The Picture

On a WordPress blog (most of the other providers allow this as well), when you add a picture to your sidebar, you have the option to add a caption to the picture. An effective caption for an informative Kindle eBook will allow a potential customer to know what your Kindle eBook is about and the price of that Kindle eBook. Here is an example that I use for my Kindle eBook, *How To Publish More Kindle eBooks Faster:*

"Learn how to **publish more eBooks faster and write 7,000 words every day** for just **$2.99**"

In one sentence, I tell potential customers what they will learn and how much it costs to gain access to the information. For your caption, you can replace what I highlighted in bold with what applies to your Kindle eBook. Listing the original price for your Kindle eBook has an additional advantage because when you run a Kindle Countdown Deal (more on this later), your customers will feel as if they got more than what they bargained for when they buy your Kindle eBook.

For fiction Kindle eBooks, you need to tell people what your fiction Kindle eBook is about in one sentence. If your Kindle eBook is about romance, then tell your potential customers that your Kindle eBook is a romantic thriller. If your Kindle eBook is about adventure, then tell your potential customers that your Kindle eBook is about an incredible journey. Choose two or three words that make your Kindle eBook sound more appealing to your potential customers. For a fiction Kindle eBook, adding the price in your caption is optional because you are not providing expertise in a fiction Kindle eBook. The entire point of a fiction Kindle eBook is to provide a good, entertaining story that has not happened in real life.

Method #3: Remove Distractions From Your Blog

Perhaps you have advertisements on other blogs. Maybe you are curious about adding advertisements on your blog, are doing research to find out how to get ads on your blog, or already have ads on your blog.

If you want to be a successful self-published author and make a full-time income from your Kindle eBooks, then you should remove those pesky ads. If you do not have ads on your blog yet, do not put them on your blog. Advertisements increase your blog's bounce rate and lead people away from your blog, and all you get is two cents. Instead of leading people away from your blog, it is more important to keep people on your blog so they see your Kindle eBooks, get curious, and eventually buy your Kindle eBooks. Whether you charge $0.99 per Kindle eBook or $9.99 per Kindle eBook, that commission is going to be better than the commission you would have gotten from an ad click.

The Only Pictures That Need To Be On Your Sidebar

The only pictures on your sidebar should be pictures of you and your products. The picture of yourself is very important because people will trust you more if they see what you look like. A classic example of where people want to see what others really look like is an online dating site. Instead of realizing on the day of the date that the person they saw on the dating site is 30 years older and doesn't have strong muscles, people on dating sites want to see what the person actually looks like. Although the consequences of not having your picture on your blog are not as bad as a dating site, your visitors will remember you based on what you look like. When you think of Niagara Falls, the Grand Canyon, or a remarkable landmark in your town, you don't think of the name. You think of what the landmark looks like. When people think of you, they don't think of your name. When they think of you, they think of what you look like in your picture on your blog's sidebar.

Method #4: Build A List Of Email Addresses

No matter what niche you are in, building a list of email addresses is critical towards your success. By building a list, you will be able to identify the people who are very likely to buy your Kindle eBooks. The best way to build a list is with a blog. On the top of your blog's sidebar should be a huge subscription box. In order to get people to subscribe to your blog, you must make it easy for people to see the subscription box. Having that huge subscription box at the top of your blog's sidebar gets the job done. If you want people to subscribe to your blog, you need to be writing quality content, offer an irresistible free prize (such as a PDF, video, or podcast), and build your blog traffic. Writing quality content is something that becomes easier with experience.

5 Ways To Get More Blog Traffic

In order to build a big list, you need more people to visit your blog. These are some ways to get more people to visit your blog:

1. **Build your presence on social networks (more on this soon).** Your followers are the people who will most likely visit your blog. Building a strong presence on social networks boosts your SEO.

2. **Include links to your older, related blog posts in your new blog posts.** This reduces your blog's bounce rate and keeps people on your blog for a longer period of time. While this does increase the likelihood of someone buying your eBook, reducing your blog's bounce rate is also good for SEO.

3. **Write guest posts.** Writing guest posts for popular blogs allows you to put your content in front of a larger audience. If the larger audience likes your content in the guest post, they will visit your blog, read the content there, and possibly subscribe to your blog for future updates.

4. **Include social sharing buttons at the bottom of your blog posts.** This is an easy way to allow your visitors to share your blog posts through their social networks. If you want your blog to spread, you must have these buttons at the bottom of your blog posts. In order to get sharing buttons on your WordPress blog, go to the settings in your dashboard and click on "sharing." Then, you will be able to play with the

options and decide which social networks your visitors can use to share your blog posts.

5. **Answer questions on Yahoo! and Wiki Answers**. Millions of questions have been posted on these two websites. If you answer the question and include a link to your blog that explains the answer, more people will visit that blog post and read your other blog posts. In addition, by answering these questions, people will recognize you as an expert.

By increasing your blog's traffic and keeping people on your blog for a longer period of time, you will be able to build your list.

Method #5: Write A Free eBook

In order to gain the trust of potential customers, you need to have a free eBook available. This free eBook should give your customer an idea of what your Kindle eBooks are like. In addition, more people are likely to buy a free eBook than they are likely to buy a paid Kindle eBook (it sounds simple, but not everyone has a free eBook available). These are the two big things that happen when you offer a free Kindle eBook:

1. **Get more positive reviews on Amazon**. If you sell the free eBook on Kindle, the people who buy that Kindle eBook are more likely to leave a positive review because there was no cost. As your free Kindle eBook gets a lot of good reviews, more people will download it, and then some of those people will buy your paid Kindle eBooks.

2. **Build your list**. If you offer a free eBook to your subscribers, more people will be enticed to enter their email address and get subscribed to your blog. As more people subscribe to your blog for the free eBook, your list will grow. When subscribers read your eBook, they will be more inclined to buy your paid Kindle eBooks. You need to make sure that your free eBook has good quality. Just because something is free doesn't mean people will automatically like it.

How To Get KDP To Sell Your eBook For $0

The process of getting KDP to sell your Kindle eBook for $0 takes a long time, but once your Kindle eBook's price goes down to $0, you will get more sales for that Kindle eBook. If you want to publish your eBook on Amazon for free, you need to publish your eBook on Kindle through KDP and also publish it with Smashwords. KDP does not let you charge anything below $0.99 for your Kindle eBook, but you can charge $0 for a Kindle eBook you publish on Smashwords. You can get that Smashwords book published on Amazon. Then, you need to get your friends to complain about the price difference. After enough people complain about the price difference, KDP will sell the Kindle eBook you published using their platform for $0. In order to find the place to complain, go to your Kindle eBook's Product Details, and at the very bottom of that section will be, "tell us about a lower price." If you get enough people to go through the process of telling Amazon about a lower price, the ecommerce giant will listen. Even if you get a lot of friends to complain, it will take at least three weeks to get the issue resolved while some issues take several months before Amazon reduces the price of your Kindle eBook.

What Your Free eBook Needs To Be About

Your free eBook needs to be similar to one of your paid Kindle eBooks. The free eBook needs to give away a lot of information, but at the end of the free eBook, you need to tell your customers that they can buy your paid Kindle eBook for more information. You can think of the free eBook as the prototype of the paid Kindle eBook. The better the free eBook is, the more likely people will buy the paid Kindle eBook that gets promoted at the end. If you have a paid Kindle eBook about blogging, you should write a shorter version of that Kindle eBook and give it to customers for free.

Method #6: Build A Targeted Following On Twitter

Twitter is a social network that allows you to interact with potential customers. The interaction can start when someone tweets a link to one of your blog posts, when someone asks you a question, or through any other conversation starter. While it is important to get more followers on Twitter, it is more important to get targeted followers.

Targeted followers are the people who are interested in what you tweet about before reading any of your tweets. That means if you tweet about social media tips, and one of your followers wants to learn more about social media before following you, that person will immediately enjoy reading your tweets. These targeted followers are also the people who will be more likely to buy your Kindle eBooks.

How To Increase Interaction

The best way to increase interaction is by being active on Twitter. Since you also have to write Kindle eBooks, I recommend only staying on Twitter for 30 minutes to at most an hour. Other ways to increase interaction are to ask questions, include pictures in your tweets, and tweet content that people would want to comment on. Although those are the tactics that will get conversations started, being active on Twitter allows those conversations to develop and lead to Kindle eBook sales.

What You Need To Be Doing For The 30-60 Minutes You Are On Twitter

There are many things that can be done on Twitter in 30-60 minutes. Some people look at trending topics during those 30-60 minutes while other users are creating an effective strategy that allows them to save time and get better results. These are the four things that you need to do for your 30-60 minutes on Twitter:

1. **Follow the followers of someone in your niche who has a lot of real followers and gains hundreds of followers every day**. Those are the targeted followers who are likely to follow you back. When these people follow you back, they will automatically be interested in the content that you tweet about. In order to save time while doing this and find people who are likely to follow you back, use Tweepi so you can easily follow other people's followers. I spend about 10 minutes on Tweepi every day.

2. **Unfollow the people who are not following you back**. When you follow people on Tweepi, not everyone will follow you. You do not want to be following hundreds of people on Tweepi every day and then have your ratio go out of control. Unfollowing the people who are not following you back will allow you to balance the ratio. However, if you follow and unfollow people too soon, Twitter will suspend your account. I tend to unfollow people who have not followed me back in 1-2 weeks. In order to save time, I use ManageFlitter which allows me to identify when I followed someone and other statistics (number of tweets, popularity, etc) as well. I spend about 10 minutes on ManageFlitter every day.

3. **Schedule tweets of your blog posts, motivational quotes, and other people's articles throughout the day**. I schedule 72 tweets every day. However, it only takes me 5 minutes to schedule that many tweets. The reason it does not take me long to schedule that many tweets is because I use HootSuite Pro. HootSuite is a free tool that allows you to schedule tweets, but for $9.99 every month, you get access to the HootSuite Pro features. One of the features is the bulk scheduler which allows me to schedule 36 tweets in 6 clicks. I repeat the process to schedule the other 36 tweets. Without HootSuite Pro, this process would take at least an hour for me to complete.

4. **Interact with your followers**. Interacting with your followers does not take a lot of time (unless someone with millions of followers gave you a

shout out). I usually spend 5-10 minutes interacting with my followers depending on how many people asked me a question, shared one of my blog posts, or started a conversation with me.

The grand total for the amount of time I spend on Twitter every day is 30-35 minutes. The only step that might eat away a lot of your time is scheduling tweets. If you have to manually schedule tweets one at a time, that will take up a lot of time. However, if you upgrade to HootSuite Pro, you will be able to save hours of your time every week.

If you spend 30-35 minutes building your presence on Twitter every day by following these tactics, you will eventually gain more than 100 followers every day. At this rate, you would have 100,000 followers in less than three years. Having more Twitter followers will boost your credibility, and as a result, more people will buy your Kindle eBooks. In addition, Twitter will allow you to grow your audience, and some of your followers will also subscribe to your blog.

Method #7: Effectively Use YouTube To Boost Sales

In order to be successful on the web, you need to have your own videos. Every successful self-published author either has their own YouTube channel or gets interviewed by other people who upload those interviews on YouTube. If your videos are really good and look professional, your customer will feel better about buying one of your Kindle eBooks.

The advantage of using YouTube is that you can upload a video on (almost) anything on a platform that gets over 1 billion visitors every month. You can upload videos where you discuss topics in your niche, and some of those videos can be specifically geared towards the topics that you discuss in your Kindle eBooks.

How To Create Awesome Videos

In order to get more sales because of YouTube, you need to create videos that your viewers will love. A good video looks professional, has the right lighting, and in that video, it is easy to tell that you are well prepared. There are few things worse on YouTube than watching someone speak off-the-cuff for 30 minutes. Speaking off-the-cuff is unprofessional and will hurt your reputation. Your reputation will not be destroyed by speaking off-the-cuff, but it won't be the same.

The best way to create better videos is to have a script in place for your videos. Better yet, use a teleprompter and have a KeyNote presentation on that teleprompter. The teleprompter can be hidden from view and can give you ideas for everything that you have to say in the video. If you decide to use a teleprompter, put it at the center of the room so you are looking straight at the person you are talking to while reading what is on the teleprompter. If the teleprompter is all the way to the left or right of the room you are in, then people will notice you turning your head to look at the teleprompter during the video.

Another easy way to make your videos better is to add special effects in the beginning, middle, and end of your videos. The best way to easily add special effects to your video is with iMovie. Special effects will keep your viewers focused so they watch your entire video.

20 Ways To Get More Subscribers On YouTube

Subscribers are critical towards your success on YouTube as well as getting more Kindle eBook sales. Subscribers are the ones who enjoy watching your content and getting notified each time you publish a new video. Getting YouTube subscribers is so important that I could not possibly make this a short list. I needed to create a giant list which is why for this part of *77 Powerful Methods To Get More Kindle eBook Sales*, I will share with you 20 ways to get more subscribers on YouTube.

1. **Upload more videos**. People will need to watch multiple videos on your channel before they decide to subscribe to your channel.

2. **Include a channel trailer**. In 1-2 minutes, tell people what kind of videos you upload on YouTube, and don't be shy to share your credentials.

3. **Tweet your videos**. By tweeting your videos and getting some of your followers to look at a couple of your videos, you will get more subscribers.

4. **Pin your videos and scatter those pins across different boards**. You can watch a YouTube video on Pinterest without leaving the social network. However, you want people to leave Pinterest so they can subscribe to your channel. In your pin's description, mention that there are more videos on your channel which you can get to by clicking on a link in the description.

5. **Have a YouTube subscribe button on your blog**. By having a YouTube subscribe button on your blog, you will be able to get a new subscriber without forcing someone to leave your blog. It's a win-win for everyone!

6. **Have a "click here to subscribe" annotation on the corner of all of your videos**. Have the annotation link to a subscription confirmation for your channel. All you need to do is paste the link in the box and from the drop down options, choose "subscribe." By doing this, anyone who clicks on the annotation automatically gets subscribed to your channel.

7. **Urge people to subscribe to your channel, but don't beg**. Urging people in the proper way can be done by saying, "If you enjoyed this video, then please subscribe to my channel which I update every week about social media, business, and blogging." Begging is just

saying, "Please, please, pretty please subscribe to my YouTube channel."

8. **Post your videos on Facebook**. Some of your friends will end up subscribing to your YouTube channel. It is important to interact with the fan base that you have already built on your other social networks (such as Facebook) in order to get more subscribers for your channel.

9. **Consistently publish videos**. If you publish videos on a consistent basis, people will notice and subscribe to your channel.

10. **Let people know when you publish your videos**. I let everyone know that I publish my videos every Saturday at 9 am Eastern Time. That means all of my subscribers (maybe not all of them) are constantly refreshing my channel every Saturday at 8:59 am Eastern Time.

11. **Share your videos on Google+**. Having a Google+ account is very helpful towards getting more YouTube subscribers. Not only do you get an entire page dedicated to all of your YouTube videos, but Google+ is also a Google-owned product that helps SEO, just like YouTube. Using Google+ to promote your YouTube channel will allow you to put the trifecta into action!

12. **Publish videos on a frequent basis**. When I decided to publish 1 YouTube video every week, I saw a dramatic increase in the number of subscribers I got for my channel. If you are publishing 1 YouTube video every week, you will give your subscribers more to watch, and they will be back for more. Publishing 1 YouTube video every year is still being consistent, but you need to combine consistency with frequency.

13. **Properly tag your videos**. Use phrases that you would want people to search for in order to find your videos. If your video is about

getting more retweets, "how to get more repins on Pinterest" would not be a good tag to use.

14. **Write good titles for your videos**. In your title, you need to tell people what your video is going to be about. The longer the title, the better. However, make sure your title is under 110 characters so people can still tweet your video using a link shortener.

15. **Write descriptions correctly**. The ideal description is one that has 2-3 paragraphs and has a link at the bottom for viewers to subscribe to your channel. You need to make sure that the people who click on this link automatically get subscribed to your channel without having to click anything else.

16. **Create quality videos**. This means creating a script, having the right lighting, and no unexpected sounds in the background.

17. **Interact with the subscribers that you already have**. The subscribers that you already have can tell their friends about you. By interacting with your subscribers, you will be getting more subscribers via word of mouth.

18. **Have a strategic channel background**. The channel background should be a picture of you at your profession or something that relates to your niche.

19. **Subscribe to other people's YouTube channels**. Some of these people will subscribe back to your channel while others will interact with you.

20. **Comment on other people's videos**. This will give you backlinks on YouTube which allows you to rank higher on YouTube's search results.

By getting more subscribers, you will be able to grow a loyal audience who watches all of your videos. As these people watch more of your videos, these people will also be more likely to buy one of your Kindle eBooks.

How To Write Effective Descriptions For Your Videos

An effective description for a video points back to your social networks and an email optin box. You want people to constantly see you on multiple places on the web so you become omnipresent. Your YouTube videos' descriptions allow that to happen. After people watch one of your YouTube videos, you need to tell them what to do next. Tell them who you are and where they go when the link in your description gets clicked on. A three paragraph description is the ideal description because it will be large enough to get someone's attention but not too large to the point where it loses attention.

Method #8: Use LinkedIn To Get Connections

LinkedIn is a social network that is all about building connections. While the ultimate goal for a conversation on a social network is to eventually turn the conversation into a series of emails, LinkedIn cuts right to the chase: all of the conversations you have with your connections are through emails. LinkedIn gives you the unique ability to go right to emails where conversations get longer, and the connections you develop become stronger.

On LinkedIn, you send invitations to people who you would like to connect with. The people who receive your invitations have the choice to either accept or ignore your request. Through my experience of connecting with other social media experts and bloggers, most people accept the invitations they receive. Just to make sure more people accept your invitation, have a good bio for your LinkedIn profile. Mention some of your accomplishments, and be sure to include some links to your Kindle eBooks.

As you build more connections on LinkedIn, you will be contacting more people through email. If you are connected with 500 people, those are 500 more people who you can urge to join your subscriber list. In order to get someone to join your subscriber list, all you need to do is have a conversation with that person and find the right time to tell them about your blog. When you tell connections about your blog, do not blatantly ask them to subscribe to your blog. Wait for the conversation to develop and then tell that person about your blog. If the person said they like your blog, then you ask that person to subscribe (but in a nice way).

Who To Connect With

You can send out a maximum of 3,000 invitations. After that, you have to contact LinkedIn and ask them to raise your limit (this does not always happen, and you should not rely on LinkedIn raising your limit). That means you can ask a maximum of 3,000 people to connect with you. With a limited amount of options, you want to make sure that the people you connect with are the right people for you. In order to determine who to connect with, here are some tips:

1. **Connect with likeminded people**. If you are a SEO expert and the person you are thinking of connecting with is an SEO expert, then you will be more likely to interact with that person. Likeminded people are a part of your target audience, and they will be likely to buy your Kindle eBooks.

2. **Connect with people who live nearby**. Emails are a powerful way to build strong connections, but there's nothing like real human interaction. By connecting with the people who live nearby, you have the option of meeting these likeminded people at a restaurant, park, clothing store, or somewhere else in your local area. People who you meet will be more likely to buy your Kindle eBook, and if any of your Kindle eBooks went physical, you can give that person a free, signed copy of your book. Giving that person your book for free will make that person feel special and more likely to buy the Kindle eBooks that you publish in the future.

3. **Connect with people who would promote you**. If you are a public speaker (or want to become one), you should connect with people who organize public speaking events that fit your niche. Connecting with these people informs them that you are here and ready to speak. By having conversations with these people while boosting your credibility with your blog, social networks, and Kindle eBooks, they may offer you a speaking opportunity. Then, when you speak to the audience, you will be able to promote your Kindle eBooks at the end of your speech.

Method #9: Use Pinterest And Instagram For Visual Content

Pinterest and Instagram are the ideal social networks to take pictures and share them with your audience. While some of these pictures need to be about your business and Kindle eBooks, some of the other pictures should be about your personal life. Many people forget to share their personal lives with potential customers. Imagine if your favorite person in your niche took pictures when he went out on vacations and posted them on Instagram. Imagine how you would feel if your favorite person in your niche took pictures and explained every day things that took place in his life. You would probably be happy to know a lot more about your favorite person in your niche.

However, there are also people who only take pictures of their personal lives. These people's only audience are their friends and relatives. Although it is good to have an audience, you want to have an audience of people who would want to buy your Kindle eBooks and become dedicated fans of what you do. Your friends can only do that to a certain extent because of the bonds of friendship, but if you add some pictures of your Kindle eBooks, you will be able to grow an audience of buyers. Friends will buy your book too, but in order to make a full-time income from your Kindle eBooks, you need to expand your audience by taking pictures of your personal life *and* your business.

As your presence grows, you will become some people's favorite person in the niche. Those people are your dedicated fans--the ones who will want to buy your new Kindle eBook before reading the description. These dedicated fans will want to learn more about your personal life to connect with you on a deeper level, and you will be able to use Pinterest and Instagram to share with people what goes on in your life when you are not writing Kindle eBooks.

These social networks can also be used to empower followers with more information about your niche. You can provide 1 tip on Instagram every day through 15 second video loops, and on Pinterest, you can create multiple boards that go into greater detail about specific parts of your niche.

Share Your Pins And Instagram Pictures On Your Other Social Networks

The people who will really appreciate your pictures are the people who are already following you. The easiest way to get more engagement for your pictures is by tapping into your other social networks. Sharing your pins and Instagram pictures on your other social networks will encourage your audiences on your other social networks to follow you on Pinterest and Instagram. As you get more followers on Pinterest and Instagram from your other social networks, these people will seek to follow you on all of your social networks. Once you get someone to follow you on two of your social networks, chances are that person will follow all of your other social network accounts as well.

How To Get Targeted Followers On Pinterest And Instagram

The tools for Pinterest and Instagram are not as advanced as Twitter tools, but the main rules are the same. Find people in your niche on Pinterest and Instagram with big followings and follow their followers. By doing this every day, you will see a consistent rise in your number of followers. Another great way to get more followers is by liking other people's pictures and pins. When you like someone's picture or pin, that person will be encouraged to follow you. When you are choosing which pictures and pins to like, you should like pictures and pins related to your niche, or the pictures and pins that you like as a person.

How Much Time You Should Be Spending On Pinterest And Instagram

For Pinterest, the amount of time you should spend on the site varies. Depending on how fast your following grows, you should spend more time on one of these social networks than the other. Ultimately, you should only be on these social networks for 20-30 minutes every day. That's enough time to post 1 picture on Instagram and send out 20 pins. You should not go over 30 minutes because then you will lose time to write your Kindle eBooks.

Method #10: Use Facebook To Make New Friends

While it is recommended to create one Facebook account for your personal life and a Facebook Page for your business, many people underestimate the power of a personal account to generate Kindle eBook sales. Having a Facebook Page does help your business, but showing people your personal Facebook account is another great way to boost your sales.

On other social networks, you simply decide whether you want to follow someone or not. On Facebook, users decide whether they want to become friends with someone or not. If someone wants to "follow" your personal account on Facebook, they send you a friend request. By accepting that friend request, the connection is more than a follower to follower connection. The connection is a friend to friend connection. Some people will care about what you do so much that they would feel honored if you accepted or send them a friend request. If you build strong connections with the people who send you friend requests on Facebook, those friends will be very likely to buy your Kindle eBooks.

How To Get More Friends On Facebook

There are numerous ways to get more friends on Facebook. Instead of going deep into all of the ways that you can get more friends on Facebook, here are some simple ways to get the job done.

1. **Build your friend list**. If you have 1,000 friends, then people who are thinking of sending you a friend request will see that you are popular. In addition, when you have more friends, those friends might tell their friends about you, and through word of mouth, you get more friends.

2. **Send friend requests to likeminded people**. Being friends with likeminded people is critical towards success. Likeminded people know and appreciate what you are doing. Likeminded people are the equivalent of targeted followers, and both of these people are the people in the world who will be more likely than any other group of people to buy your Kindle eBooks. Likeminded people may even ask what your next Kindle eBook is about and how much progress you have made on it so far.

3. **Go through the friend lists of likeminded people**. By going through the friend lists of likeminded people, you will be able to discover more likeminded people. When using this strategy, I recommend leap frogging among multiple accounts of likeminded people. You do want to connect

with more likeminded people, but you don't want to look like a stalker either.

4. **Become Facebook friends with your friends in real life**. Ask your friends if they have a Facebook account (since over 1 billion people have Facebook accounts, chances are your friend has one). Then, become friends with that person on Facebook. This is the simplest way to build your list of Facebook friends, but you will be amazed with how many extra friends you can get with this tactic.

Method #11: Create A Facebook Page

Having a personal Facebook account is important, but having a Facebook Page for your business is just as important. Having a Facebook Page gives you a place to tell people about your upcoming Kindle eBooks and share your blog posts. Facebook provides deeper analytics for Facebook Pages than personal accounts. Those analytics include how many people in your audience are on Facebook at any hour for all seven days of the week. In addition, people will be able to see how many people liked your Facebook Page. The more likes your Facebook Page has, the more credible you will become. If your Facebook Page eventually reaches 1,000 likes, the people who visit your Facebook Page will believe that you know a lot about dominating Facebook and are a top expert in your niche. There are several questions that come up with a Facebook Page. Some people are quick to point to Facebook's declining user base while others are quick to point out how difficult it is to establish a strong presence on Facebook. It is important to remember that Facebook still has over 1 billion users, and the only reason most people think it is difficult to create a successful Facebook page is because they do not know how. The advantage of having a successful Facebook Page is that Facebook is a social network that encourages oversharing. All it takes to share something is the click of a button. Then, more people see your post. If 5,000 people like your Facebook post, chances are over 50,000 people are going to see your post. Then, more people continue liking your post and it continues to spread. The only way to go that viral on Facebook is by optimizing your Facebook Page.

Update It Four Times Every Day

Updating your Facebook Page four times every day is not enough to take too much time away from your writing. However, updating your Facebook Page four times every day allows enough people to see your post so it can spread. You can use Facebook or HootSuite to schedule all of your posts in the evening (or any time of day to your preference) so you don't have to worry about your Facebook Page the next day. You don't have to be on Facebook every day in order for something to get posted on your Facebook Page every day.

Get More People To Like Your Facebook Page

There are three good options to getting more likes for your Facebook Page. The first and easiest option is asking your friends to like your Facebook Page. This is the best strategy to get short-term likes for your Facebook Page. If you have 100 friends on your profile, you may be able to get 10-20 likes right away. If you have 1,000 friends, then you may be able to get 100 likes right away. There is no harm in asking your friends to like your Facebook Page. The worst they can do is say no.

The second option is to create a strong presence on the web and get more likes that way. This is the best strategy to get long-term likes for your Facebook Page. The people with over 100,000 likes on their Facebook Pages are the ones with powerful presences on the web. In addition, if you have a powerful presence on the web, more people are going to share your Facebook Page's posts.

The third and final option is to use Facebook Advertising. Facebook Advertising is a nice transition point between asking your friends to like your page and building a strong presence on the web. Depending on how much money you have to spend, Facebook Advertising can get you thousands of extra likes. Although there are some people who are skeptical towards Facebook Advertising, it is a great way to make you look important on Facebook and gradually build a targeted audience. Facebook Advertising is something that you should only rely on for a short amount of time, not forever.

10 Additional Methods To Get People To Like Your Facebook Page
It is important to have as many methods as possible to get more likes for your Facebook Page. Here are 10 additional methods that will allow you to get more likes.

1. **Post consistently**. People need to see you as an active user on Facebook in order to remember who you are and go back to your page often.
2. **Host weekly contests that require likes in order to participate**. People will like your page to be a part of the giveaway, and soon some of that person's friends will also want to be a part of the giveaway. You can giveaway your product (book, training course, etc) and get more likes at the same time!
3. **Build your following**. The bigger your following is, the more likes you will get. Hosting successful contests is a great way to grow your following on Facebook.
4. **Post what your fans like**. If your fans are into social media, posting interesting articles about social media will get more likes.
5. **Embed Facebook posts on your blog**. More people will be able to see your post, and as a result more people will like your post.

6. **Post videos**. There are some videos that are getting hundreds of thousands of likes on Facebook.
7. **Use humor whenever possible**. If you give someone a good laugh, they are more likely to click the like button.
8. **Post random facts that are still relevant to your page**. If your page is about social media, posting a daily social media statistic will get the job done.
9. **Post infographics**. Infographics are very popular on the web, and most people read the entire infographic because it comes text with pictures.
10. **Post inspirational quotes**. Those always get liked on Facebook and shared on any other social network as well.

What To Post On Your Facebook Page

Your Facebook Page is a big part of your business. That means 80% of the content you post on your Facebook Page needs to be related to your niche. People who view your Facebook Page need to know what it is all about. A bio does a good job at explaining what your Facebook Page is about, but your posts on your page need to support what your bio says. By staying constant with your niche, people who visit your Facebook Page from your blog will be more likely to like your page. It is important to stay consistent with your niche across all of your social networks.

You should also include pictures in your posts. Facebook posts with pictures get more engagement than Facebook posts without pictures. That's because a picture gets noticed more than regular text. If you are talking about Twitter, include a picture of the logo. If you are talking about baseball players, include a picture of the baseball diamond. Depending on what your Facebook Page is about, you may also find time to squeeze in some motivational quotes. Some motivational quotes get over 2,000 likes and generate a lot of traffic to those people's Facebook Pages.

Method #12: Generate The Push You Need To Boost Sales

Many self-published authors wonder why their Kindle eBooks are not getting sold even when those Kindle eBooks are on Amazon, the world's largest ecommerce site. I'm sure there were self-published authors who did the math for how many sales they would make if 1% or even 0.01% of people who visit Amazon every day bought their Kindle eBooks.

Sadly, many self-published authors realize that Amazon is not going to promote their new Kindle eBooks the way Amazon promotes bestsellers. This is the point when most self-published authors give up. If you have not given up at this stage, and you know you want to continue writing Kindle eBooks, there is no reason for you to give up now. Generating the push is the next step towards boosting your sales.

You are probably wondering how to generate the push, what happens when the push gets carried out, and what the push is in the first place. All you need to do to generate the push is implement Methods 1 to 11. The push comes from your blog, social networks, and subscriber list. After you generate a strong push, Amazon will start to promote your Kindle eBook. Your Kindle eBook will appear in more "Customers Also Bought" sections and will rank higher on Amazon's search engine (Amazon's search engine is the 4th largest on the web). Generating the push is like pushing a snowball down an endless hill--once you do all of the hard work (pushing the snowball down the hill), Amazon appreciates your hard work by letting the snowball go down the hill uninterrupted--at least for a while.

As long as you continue to grow your blog, social networks, and subscriber list, Amazon will continue to promote your Kindle eBook. Once Amazon starts to promote your Kindle eBook, it is very easy to have it remain that way.

Summarizing Methods 1-12

Amazon only promotes the Kindle eBooks that are making a lot of sales. If you want Amazon to promote your Kindle eBooks, then you need to grow an audience of people who will buy your Kindle eBooks. Methods 1 to 11 explain how you can grow your presence with a blog, a subscriber list, and social networks. The only problem with the first 11 methods is that these methods can take a lot of time to implement. Implementing these first 11 methods will not allow you to see a dramatic short-term change, but the long-term change in your sales will be extraordinary.

Method #12 serves to emphasize how important the other 11 methods are. An overwhelming majority of popular self-published authors also have popular blogs, big subscriber lists, and over 10,000 followers on a social network. Method #12 also reveals that in order to become a successful self-published author, most of your sales have to come through Amazon. Once Amazon starts to promote your Kindle eBook, Amazon will promote your Kindle eBook to hundreds of thousands of people who search for your book's keywords (more on the keywords later).

Methods 13-25: Creating The Kindle eBook

There are many components that go into the Kindle eBook itself to decide whether someone buys it or not. You need to create the ideal Kindle eBook that people in your target audience would want to buy. Although content is a big part of how well your Kindle eBook does, there are other components that decide how many sales your Kindle eBook gets.

Method #13: Write Quality Content

Writing quality content is the most important part of getting returning customers. Regardless of whether you have published 1 Kindle eBook or 10 Kindle eBooks, all of those Kindle eBooks must contain quality content. The right content will show your customers that they got what they paid for. By having the content that makes customers realize they got what they paid for, those customers will buy more of your Kindle eBooks.

In addition to getting more returning customers, your Kindle eBooks will also get more positive reviews. Positive reviews are essential towards boosting your sales. If you had to either buy a Kindle eBook with an average of 3 stars after 100 reviews or a Kindle eBook at the same price about the same topic with an average of 4.6 stars after 100 reviews, which one would you buy? Chances are you would buy the Kindle eBook with better reviews. Writing quality content allows you to get more of those positive reviews.

The most important thing that quality content does is boost your credibility in your niche. When you boost your credibility, customers will have a strong belief that every Kindle eBook you write contains quality content. This belief leads to returning customers, and all you need to do to get these customers to come back again and again is to continue delivering on your promise to provide quality content.

Is Content King?

There has been a dispute over the years about whether content or traffic is king. Some people argue that quality content does not go noticed unless there is a lot of traffic. These people argue that getting a lot of traffic is more important then writing good content. Whether you are siding with content or traffic, here is the way you need to look at them.

Quality content is essential towards success and increases the likelihood of returning customers. Although getting traffic is also very important, leading visitors to a low quality Kindle eBook will not boost your sales. If anything, it will boost the amount of refunds you get for your Kindle eBook. What you need to focus on first is writing the quality content. What you need to do after that is get the traffic. By following this method, the people who visit your Kindle eBook's page will be happy with the quality. You can get a lot of traffic, but if the visitors are not happy with what they see, then there's no point for the visitor to stick around. Quality content is the primary reason why your visitor would want to stick around and possibly buy your Kindle eBook.

Method #14: Write About Topics That Interest You

It is very important to write about the topics that interest you instead of the mainstream topics. Celebrity gossip is mainstream in the news, but if you write a Kindle eBook about celebrity gossip and don't know much about it, your customers will notice. Your Kindle eBook will not be able to go in depth about celebrities because you don't know a lot about celebrity gossip. One of the worst things to get noticed for is not knowing a lot about your niche, and getting noticed for this reason will without a doubt decrease your credibility. The worst part is that it also takes longer to write a Kindle eBook about a topic you do not fully understand. If you have to do extensive research about your Kindle eBook's topic from the very beginning, that's a recipe for disaster.

The solution is to write about topics that interest you. When a topic interests you, you must remember that you need to write at least 15,000 words about it. That is a lot of words, but that is what it takes to write a 45-50 page Kindle eBook. You need to be writing about the same topic for weeks in order to finish a Kindle eBook that you would want to self-publish and call your own. For nonfiction writers, the topics that interest you must also be topics that you know about. The more expertise you have in a certain area, the better your content in that Kindle eBook will be.

Method #15: Focus On One Niche

You may have several interests. You may know a lot about sports, blogging, home cleaning, and other things as well. However, you need to focus on one niche. You need to build an authority around a single niche so people know you as an expert in that area. In addition, focusing on one niche increases the likelihood of returning customers. If you write one Kindle eBook about sports, another one about animals, and a third one about home cleaning, you will not get as many returning customer. However, if you write one Kindle eBook about mammals, another one about amphibians, and a third one about reptiles, then you are more likely to get returning customers. Since your Kindle eBooks focus on one niche (in this case, animals), you will be able to get more returning customers.

Writing Kindle eBooks Becomes Easier Over Time

If you implement Method #14, writing each Kindle eBook will be easier than the last one. After you write each of your Kindle eBooks, you will have more knowledge about your niche which you can use when you write your next Kindle eBook. Then, the process continues for as long as you let it continue.

You Will Become The Go-To Expert In Your Niche

No matter how hard you try, there is no way to become an expert of all trades. There are going to be certain niches that you are not an expert in. The only option you have left is becoming the go-to expert in a particular niche--your niche. By becoming the go-to expert in your niche, people will visit your blog and social networks to read your content and ask for advice. Being the go-to expert in your niche also boosts your credibility. If you are the go-to expert in your niche, customers will have a strong belief that your Kindle eBooks are better than the competition. This strong belief will make potential customers more likely to buy your Kindle eBooks because these potential customers have a strong belief that they are buying top class Kindle eBooks.

Method #16: Make Sure Your Kindle eBook Solves A Problem That Your Target Audience Cares About

There are many problems your target audience has. If your target audience is people who want to build their presence on social media, these people will want to know how they can boost engagement, gain followers, and get their followers to share their posts among other things as well. Whether your target audience cares about growing their presence on social media or not, your target audience has problems that **you** can solve. The reason why someone becomes a go-to expert of their niche is because people recognize that person has more knowledge about their niche than most of the people in that niche. That is why people pursue the go-to experts for help. Being an expert in your niche shows that you know more than most of the people in your target audience. You know the solutions, and your target audience needs them.

Think of it this way. Your target audience is taking a final exam in molecular biology, and you have the best study guide around. Giving the best study guide to your target audience would help them study for the exam and get a better grade. Having the study guide gives people in your target audience an advantage; new knowledge. The new knowledge some readers obtain from Kindle eBooks consists of health tips while other Kindle eBooks give readers an advantage in their niche. In essence, you are helping the reader to get from Point A to Point B in a shorter amount of time.

Go Through The Questions People Ask You

When you become the go-to expert in your niche, more people will ask you questions. While it does take longer to answer one question at a time, those questions are questions that other people in your target audience have as well. The only difference is that one person in your target audience (or a few) decided to speak up about the problem while others must do the research on their own to come up with an answer. As you get asked more questions, patterns will emerge. Some questions will get asked more than others. The popular questions can inspire some of your future Kindle eBooks that goes into great detail about the answer to that particular question.

If it is a popular question, you can summarize the answer and tell the person who asked the question that you recently published an entire Kindle eBook that deals with this specific problem. That way, people in your targeted audience will buy your Kindle eBook to solve their problems, and then Amazon promotes your Kindle eBook. In the end, you get to grow your audience just by answering one question in 15,000 or more words.

Method #17: Write Good Titles, Subtitles, and Chapter Names

The title and subtitle for your Kindle eBook are critical factors that decide how many sales that Kindle eBook gets. In order to boost your sales, you must have an attention grabbing title and subtitle. The title needs to explain what your Kindle eBook is about in a few words, and the subtitle must support the title.

Seth Godin is a very successful author. All of the books he publishes almost automatically become bestsellers. One of the books that he published that really launched his career was *Purple Cow*. Although *Purple Cow* is an intriguing title, it is not about a purple cow who goes on an adventure. *Purple Cow* is a business book, and the only reason potential customers know that is because the subtitle says, "Transform Your Business By Being Remarkable." The subtitle strengthens the title's message and makes it clear about what is being discussed in *Purple Cow*.

What Kind Of Subtitles Work?

Each Kindle eBook has a different set of subtitles that work. A nonfiction book about baseball and a fiction book about knights and dragons are going to have different subtitles. The best option you have is to write a clear and catchy subtitle that supports a clear and catchy title. For a How-To book, you need to identify what type of content you are going to provide for your readers. If your customers do not know what they are buying, then they won't buy the product in the first place. A confused customer never buys. Your subtitle must be longer than your title. Having a big title makes word of mouth difficult. Imagine telling someone about the book *Purple Cow*. That's easy because there are only two words in the title. In addition, a title like *Purple Cow* stands out from the other books. However, talking to your friends about a book called *Transform Your Business By Being*

Remarkable is a little harder. That's 6 words, and that title does not sound nearly as remarkable as *Purple Cow*.

When The Chapters Come Into Play

Once your title and subtitle get the customer's attention, they may look inside your Kindle eBook with the free previewer. When a customer looks inside your Kindle eBook, they must be able to see all of the chapters in your Kindle eBook. Your chapters need to stand out, be catchy, and be clear. Do not name your chapters the way everyone else names their chapters. If you would expect to find your chapter in any How-To book in your niche or any novel similar to yours, try to call it something else. When customers think of buying a Kindle eBook, they want to see chapter names that deviate from the norm and identify what the content in those chapters will discuss.

Method #18: Include A Table Of Contents In Your Kindle eBook With Hyperlinks

Customers want to see a table of contents so they know what they are getting when they buy your Kindle eBook. A majority of bestselling authors give their readers a table of contents so the reader has a small outline of the Kindle eBook. This allows the potential customers to know what kinds of topics are getting discussed in the Kindle eBook. You can come up with catchy chapter names, but potential customers won't know about any of them unless they can see a Table of Content in the free preview.

Why You Need To Add Hyperlinks To Your Chapter Titles

The advantage of a Kindle eBook over a physical book is that you can use hyperlinks. Hyperlinks are links that readers can click on to be redirected to another page in your Kindle eBook. Instead of a reader flipping pages to find the chapter, you can give your readers a hyperlink to the chapter in the table of contents. When someone clicks on the hyperlink, they get sent to the page with the chapter.

For people with a Mac Book, these are the steps you need to take in order to create hyperlinks for Pages on Mac.

1. Highlight the content you want to lead readers to (i.e. The name of your chapter).
2. Go to the inspector (the "i" at the right corner).
3. Click on the link option (the white arrow in the blue circle).
4. Go to the Bookmark section and press the "+" sign. Now you have created the bookmark
5. Go to your table of contents and find the name of the same chapter. Then, highlight it.
6. Repeat steps 2-3
7. Go to the hyperlink section, click on the blank square next to "Enable as a hyperlink."
8. For "Link to," select bookmark.
9. Then, find and select the bookmark that you saved earlier in Step 4.

You now have a hyperlink in your table of contents that leads to the chapter of your Kindle eBook right when the hyperlink gets clicked. Hyperlinks makes the reading experience better because it allows your readers to go to certain sections of your book at a faster rate. The more convenient you can make the reading experience for your readers, the more they will like your Kindle eBook, leave a good review, and become returning customers.

Method #19: Publish More Kindle eBooks

There is strength in numbers. By publishing more Kindle eBooks, your customers will have more options. If you publish Kindle eBooks about getting the right amount of sleep, eating healthier, and becoming smarter, your customer only has to like and buy one of the three Kindle eBooks for you to get the sale. Let's say your customer bought the Kindle eBook about eating healthier. If you only stopped at the Kindle eBook about getting the right amount of sleep, you would not have made the sale with the health Kindle eBook.

If you went into a clothing store, and it only had one type of clothing, you would either buy that clothing or walk right out of the store. The problem with this business model is that when people get presented with that option, many people walk out. All it takes is the shirt to be the wrong size. There are other factors such as the color or style of the clothing that influences whether people buy from that store or not. If clothing stores only offered one option, they would not be successful. That is why the successful clothing stores offer hundreds of options. It seems as if right when one shelf of clothing has no good options, the next shelf has plenty of good options (that's why people get trapped at TJ Maxx). Whether you are looking for dresses, blazers, or shorts, it seems as if clothing stores have something for (almost) everyone.

You need to present your potential customers with as many options as you possibly can in order to boost your sales. Self-published authors almost never become successful by only selling 1 Kindle eBook. Instead, they write and self-publish multiple Kindle eBooks. Most of the successful self-published authors have self-published over 10 Kindle eBooks while others have written more than 25 Kindle eBooks. The more options you provide for your customers, the more likely they are to buy one of your Kindle eBooks. If someone buys one of your 25 Kindle eBooks, it still counts as a sale, and chances are that person will come back.

The Math Behind Making $100,000 Every Year

Math gets applied in the real world in more ways than we know. One of those methods is identifying the number of sales someone would need to make $100,000 every year. Since most self-published authors sell their Kindle eBooks for $2.99, I decided to calculate how many Kindle eBooks these self-published authors would have to sell in order to make $100,000 every year. Assuming that each Kindle eBook brings in an average of $2.02 per sale (the real number will be slightly higher or lower depending on the file size of your Kindle eBook), these are the numbers:

1. 49,505 sales every year
2. 4,125 sales every month
3. 138 sales every day

When looking at these numbers for the first time, they may look impossible to reach. However, reaching these numbers is possible. Many self-published authors already get these numbers, and there is no reason why you can't get these numbers too.

Those numbers look big, but every Kindle eBook you publish cuts down the amount of sales all of your Kindle eBooks have to make in order to make $100,000 every year.

This is what happens to the numbers when you publish a second Kindle eBook:

1. 24,753 sales every year for both Kindle eBooks
2. 2,063 sales every month for both Kindle eBooks
3. 69 daily sales every day for both Kindle eBooks

Those numbers still might look scary, but they don't look nearly as scary as the other numbers. Most of the successful self-published authors have published 10 Kindle eBooks at $2.99 each. These are the last numbers, but these numbers show the possibilities of being a full-time self-published author.

1. 4,951 sales every year for each of the 10 Kindle eBooks

2. 413 sales every month for each of the 10 Kindle eBooks

3. 14 sales every day for each of the 10 Kindle eBooks

Getting 14 sales every day for 10 Kindle eBooks sounds much easier than getting one of your Kindle eBooks to make 138 sales every day. It is, and publishing more Kindle eBooks will make those numbers get smaller. The smaller you make those numbers, the more likely you are to make $100,000 every year from your Kindle eBooks. The only way to make those numbers smaller is by self-publishing more Kindle eBooks.

Returning Customers And The Three Sales Rule

Immediately when you publish your second Kindle eBook, you are giving yourself a big advantage in the Kindle marketplace. Unlike the self-published authors who have only published 1 Kindle eBook, you can get returning customers. If you publish a Part 2 for one of your Kindle eBooks, the people who bought and liked your first Kindle eBook tend to buy the second one too.

One of the rules to making sales is that once someone buys three of your Kindle eBooks, that customer will buy all of your future Kindle eBooks. That means as more people buy three of your Kindle eBooks, you will have more customers ready to buy your next Kindle eBook right when it gets published. In fact, some of them will probably have the date of your next Kindle eBook circled on their calendar.

More Virtual Shelf Space

When you publish more Kindle eBooks, you are giving yourself more shelf space. Although Kindle eBooks are digital, you need to envision all of the Kindle eBooks on a real-life bookshelf. That would be a giant bookshelf, and it is in this bookshelf where most Kindle eBooks get no attention. As you self-publish more Kindle eBooks, you will increase the number of

Kindle eBooks you have on that colossal bookshelf. The more Kindle eBooks you have throughout the bookshelf, the bigger your audience will become. If you go to your local library, you are more likely to encounter a book written by an author who has 10 books in the library than you are to encounter a book written by an author who only has 1 book in the library.

Method #20: Consistently And Frequently Publish Kindle eBooks

Consistent is one of my favorite words. Publishing a Kindle eBook is not as hard as it sounds. Publishing Kindle eBooks consistently and frequently is not as easy of a feat to attempt, but attempting and successfully implementing this method will allow you to get more long-term sales. The three sales rule is a powerful way to boost your sales for future Kindle eBooks. However, if you go inactive for several months, people will forget about you, and your Kindle eBook sales will see a gradual decline. This is what happened to me a while ago because I decided to focus more of my attention on my blog and social media. In addition, I finished a book that I wrote in August 2013 but published it in December because it was a book with business tips for 2014. I did not want to publish that book in August because no one would be thinking about 2014. After I published that Kindle eBook, I lost my way and forgot how to write thousands of words every day. It took me four months to get back into the groove and publish another Kindle eBook. Another reason I was inactive was because I gave myself deadlines that were too long. I currently write over 30,000 words every week, but I did not write anything close to that for the giant book I was working on. I knew I had given myself a deadline that was too long, but I also noticed a decline in my sales. Noticing the decline gave me the motivation to do more research on successful self-published authors. I quickly learned that these self-published authors publish their Kindle eBooks at a rate that beats the traditional publishing system. While some successful self-published authors are publishing one Kindle eBook every 6 weeks, others are publishing one Kindle eBook every 3 weeks.

By consistently and frequently publishing Kindle eBooks, the numbers mentioned in Method #19 get reduced at a faster rate. Publishing Kindle eBooks consistently is only one piece of the puzzle. Consistency can mean self-publishing 1 Kindle eBook every 3 week or publishing 1 Kindle eBook every year. They are both consistent, but one is better than the other. This is why you need to publish Kindle books at a consistent, frequent rate. If you have never published a single Kindle eBook, but you get started today and publish 1 Kindle book every 3 weeks, you would publish 10 Kindle eBooks in 7 and a half months. That's how long it would take for a new self-published author to mathematically be able to make $100,000 every year if all of his Kindle eBooks got 14 sales each.

Is It Possible To Be Successful By Self-Publishing 1 Kindle eBook Every Year?

It is possible to become successful while self-publishing 1 Kindle eBook every year, but the chances are very, very unlikely. If you wanted to be successful by self-publishing 1 Kindle eBook every year, you would need a ginormous email list of active people (my guess would be at least 10,000 people), have close to 1 million followers on all of your social networks combined, and write 200+ page Kindle eBooks with better information in them than every other self-published author in your niche.

To sum it up, as you publish more Kindle eBooks every year, you will get closer to the six figure club. The quicker you can publish your Kindle eBooks (while ensuring quality), the more likely you are to become successful. The minimum rate you need to publish Kindle eBooks at is 6 weeks. If you are able to publish 1 Kindle eBook every 3-5 weeks, then that's even better. The more Kindle eBooks you publish, the more sales you will be able to get. Your sales will rise exponentially as you continue to publish more Kindle eBooks and implement the methods in this book.

Method #21: Have A Cool Cover

Having a cool cover is one of the most underrated ways to make more sales. Most self-published authors know that having a cool cover has some kind of an effect on sales, but the effect a cool cover has is ginormous. Although "Don't judge a book by its cover" is a common phrase that we get taught at a very young age, people are constantly judging a book by its cover. You probably judge a book by its cover without realizing. The bestselling Kindle eBooks have great content, but they just so happen to have cool looking covers to go with the content. The cool cover grabs the customer's attention, and then it is up to the Kindle eBook's content to win the customer over.

Since we judge books by their covers, we make assumptions about the content in the book. Customers will think that a Kindle eBook with a sloppy cover also contains sloppy content. This is not the message that you want any of your potential customers to receive by looking at your Kindle eBook's cover. However, if your cover is a cool one, customers will think that your Kindle eBook contains quality content. Once your customers come to the realization that your Kindle eBook contains quality content, those customers will be more likely to buy your Kindle eBook. All you have to do is provide the quality content so that the customers you get feel happy about their purchases.

How To Get A Cool Cover Without Stealing A Picture On The Web

The big problem with getting a cool cover is that most of the cool pictures on the web are copyrighted or watermarked. Taking that picture and making it the cover of your Kindle eBook goes against the copyright, and if you get caught, that would ruin the reputation you worked hard for. Not only would you have to take the cover down, but you would have to get a new one as quickly as possible. That can mean using another copyright protected picture, and a series of violations will damage your reputation as a self-published author.

Instead of stealing someone else's work, some people use a default cover. Although the Cover Creator is a free option, the default covers do not look cool. These covers are not the ones that say, "Pick me! Pick me!" to the customer. There are many Kindle eBooks with these types of covers, and none of those covers pop out to potential customers.

If you want the best cover for your Kindle eBook, then you should hire someone to get the job done for you. There is no reason for you to learn photoshop, photo editing, or anything similar just to make the cover of your next Kindle eBook. Hiring other people will give you an image you can use, make your Kindle eBook look professional, and gives you more time to write content. It does not cost a lot of money to get a professional Kindle eBook cover. On Fiverr, you can get a good looking Kindle eBook cover for just $5. That is all it takes to get the kind of cover that may double, triple, or even quadruple your sales. You may have to pay $5 for the cover, but the investment will pay itself off in a few sales. For a $2.99 Kindle book, it would only take 3 sales to cover the $5 expense. In fact, a cool cover might get you thousands of sales that you would have never gotten with a cover from Cover Creator. The cost for a cover is small, but the return investment will be huge.

Method #22: Make Your Cover Look Great In The "Customers Also Bought" Section

Many of the people who buy Kindle eBooks first see them in the "Customers Bought" section. Your Kindle eBook's cover may look cool, but you also want your Kindle eBook's cover to look cool in the "Customers Also Bought" sections. How good does your picture look 90 by 125 pixels wide? Can people still see the title? These are both important when people see your Kindle eBook in the "Customers Also Bought" section.

Your smaller picture and title in Amazon's sections must encourage the customer to click the link to your Kindle eBook. When that happens, the customer gets to see your cool cover as a bigger picture and a description of your Kindle eBook. After a potential customer clicks on the link, you have their full attention.

How To Make Your Cover Look Great In Amazon's Sections

When you hire someone to create your cover, you need to be specific with the pixels and design. Always assume that person needs to know the tiniest detail. Tell them your title, subtitle, and author name word for word. If the person you hire has only made a few Kindle eBook covers, remind that person that customers must also be able to see the title when the picture of your Kindle eBook's cover is 90 to 125 pixels wide.

Adding this important detail will let these people know what they need to do when they make your Kindle eBook cover. In my experience, asking this request does not cost any extra money. As the customer, you have the right to tell the cover designer everything that you want. Telling them about your Kindle eBook's picture being 90 to 125 pixels wide is essential.

Method #23: Make Your Kindle eBooks Longer

Another great way to boost your sales is by making your Kindle eBooks longer. If there are two nonfiction how-to Kindle eBooks about the same topic at the same price, and one of them is 30 pages while the other is 150 pages, most customers will purchase the longer Kindle eBook because it contains more information. Most of the bestselling Kindle eBooks have well over 100 pages. Writing 15,000 words is the minimum for writing a Kindle eBook, writing more words will show your customers that they are getting more for their money. Writing 45,000 words will definitely allow you to exceed 100 pages and show your customers that they are getting a lot of information in your Kindle eBook.

Warning! Quality Content Is Still Super Important

Although making your Kindle eBooks longer is a great way to boost your sales, quality content is still super important. It is possible to write an amazing Kindle eBook in 45,000 words, but it is equally possible to write a low quality Kindle eBook in 45,000 words. A low quality Kindle eBook will get bad reviews, and that damages the likelihood of that Kindle eBook getting future sales. It becomes more difficult to recover as the bad reviews stockpile in the beginning. That is why you still need to write quality content so those bad reviews do not stockpile.

Making your Kindle eBooks longer is definitely something worth looking into. Your Kindle eBooks should be at least 50 pages long in order to show customers that there is a lot of content in your Kindle eBooks. While some of those Kindle eBooks may go under 50 pages, your goal should be to make sure that most of your Kindle eBooks exceed 50 pages.

How To Write More Words Every Day

If you decide to write longer Kindle eBooks, you will want to know how you can write more words every day. I wrote an entire Kindle eBook about this called *How To Publish More Kindle eBooks Faster*, but I will give you a condensed summary of that Kindle eBook. These are the things you need to do to write more words every day.

1. **Wake up earlier**. If you wake up 1 hour earlier every day, then you have 1 extra hour to write content for your Kindle eBooks.

2. **Give yourself bigger goals**. Writing 500 words every day is an easy goal. Writing 7,000 words every day is not as easy. The bigger goal will force you to put more time into writing.

3. **Give yourself closer deadlines**. You will be more productive if you have to write a Kindle eBook in 6 weeks than you would if you have to write a Kindle eBook in 6 months.

4. **Proofread your manuscript the right way**. While some people proofread a manuscript just to find more mistakes, other people also read the manuscript to find topics in the book to expand on. This is also an easy way to add more words to your Kindle eBook (but make sure those words are good).

5. **Love the topics that you write about**. It will be easy for you to write about the topics you enjoy.

Those are 5 ways to write more words every day. By implementing these tactics, you will find the time to write 45,000 word Kindle eBooks in the same amount of time it would take for most people to write a 20,000 word Kindle eBook.

Method #24: Proofread Your Kindle eBook

Proofreading is the step of publishing that most self-published authors skip over. No matter how good you think your content is, chances are there are typos throughout your Kindle eBook. There are only two ways that you will learn about typos in your Kindle eBooks:

1. **If you proofread your manuscript (recommended).**

2. **If the person who gave you a 1 star review mentions typos (not recommended).**

You do not want to get a 1 star review just because you made typos and did not proofread your manuscript before publishing your Kindle eBook.

That would be a careless way to get a bad review. In addition, reviews during the early stage are critical. If the first review you get is a 1 star review, then potential customers would be scared away by your Kindle eBook's average number of stars. The first review represents the average. Getting a good review will increase your chances of selling more Kindle eBooks while a bad review will decrease the likelihood of you selling more Kindle eBooks. Proofreading early allows you to avoid all of the heartache later.

How You Need To Think Of Proofreading
Many people only see proofreading as a way to identify typos and make the entire manuscript grammatically correct. While it is important for the entire manuscript to be grammatically correct, it is also important for you to expand on certain concepts in your Kindle eBook. When I first published my Kindle eBook *Keep The Ball Rolling*, it was only 18 pages long (I published it during my second month as a self-published author, so I didn't know better). Although the book initially attracted customers, the Kindle eBook's popularity declined as it became an old title.

After I learned that an 18 page Kindle eBook was way too short, I knew I had to step it up. The 18 page Kindle eBook was a little over 8,000 words. Instead of writing about more topics, I decided to proofread the entire manuscript for a second time. I found no typos (because that's what I previously checked the manuscript for). Instead, I looked for ideas that I could expand upon. In just one day, I was able to expand on multiple ideas and add an extra 4,000 words to *Keep The Ball Rolling*. In one day, that Kindle eBook went from having 18 pages to having 32 pages. Proofreading has the potential to make your Kindle eBooks longer than they already are. If you couldn't think of any more topics, your Kindle eBook has 39,000 words, and you really wanted to reach 40,000 words, don't get disappointed. You can reach the 40,000 word milestone when you proofread your Kindle eBook.

Your Published Kindle eBooks Can Always Get Updated

My entire experience of proofreading *Keep The Ball Rolling* taught me that any published Kindle eBook can still be updated. Just because you published your Kindle eBook does not mean you never have the power to update it ever again. After publishing 10 Kindle eBooks, you may realize that your first Kindle eBook needs to be updated. Like I did, you may realize that one of your Kindle eBooks is too short. You may have used an unprofessional cover for one of your first Kindle eBooks, and now that you are making extra revenue, you will now have the knowledge and resources needed to get a better cover for your Kindle eBook. When you update a Kindle eBook, you will be providing a better experience for your readers.

Method #25: Use HARO To Get Sources For Your Kindle eBooks

You can use HARO (Help A Reporter Out) to submit content for someone's question and/or to ask your own questions. Submitting a question related to your Kindle eBook will allow you to connect with more people and feature them in it. Featuring people in your Kindle eBook has two positive effects. The first positive effect is that your Kindle eBook grows in length. As always, quality content is essential, but the length of your Kindle eBook also has an impact on sales. The second positive effect is that the people who you featured in your Kindle eBook are going to up it. Buying the Kindle eBook gives these people a chance to boost their ego. One day, my uncle showed me a book that had Bill Gates in the book's index (many books do). Then, he showed me his name in the same book's index. He flipped to the page number very quickly and showed me the paragraph he got featured in. Then, he had me read the entire part of the book where he was featured. Imagine having 50 people do that with your Kindle eBook to all of their friends. Who wouldn't show off that you mentioned them in your Kindle eBook? Better yet, publish this Kindle eBook as a paperback so it is easier for these people to show themselves (and your book) off to their friends. Then, that person's friends will be very likely to buy your book.

More Sales On Launch Day

The people who get featured in your Kindle eBook will want to buy your Kindle eBook as soon as it gets published. If you feature 50 people in your Kindle eBook, chances are 40 of these people will buy your book on the day it launches. Buying the Kindle eBook boosts their ego and gives them the power to show it off to their friends.

More Five Star Reviews

The people who you feature in your Kindle eBook will easily give your Kindle eBook a five star review. Since you already have their email addresses from HARO, you will easily be able to contact these people and ask them if they would like to leave a review for your Kindle eBook. These people will be very inclined to leave you five star reviews since their name is in your Kindle eBook. As you get more five star reviews, your Kindle eBook will look more credible. Now it just comes down to providing your customers with quality content.

This Requires A Lot Of Work

Although the rewards of using HARO to get sources and write your Kindle eBook are high, it takes a lot of effort. If you want to feature 50 people in your Kindle eBook, you need to send enough queries to find 50 suitable responses. Before finding the suitable responses, you need to read through all of the responses (good or bad). After you find the suitable responses, you still need to contact these people and ask them questions. In some cases, you may even have to perform an interview via Skype or phone. Finally, you will have to take all of this information and write a few hundred words about 50 different people. This is a very time consuming process, but it is well worth it. If you have the money, there is another option.

Hire Assistants To Do This For You

As you start to get more sales for your Kindle eBooks, you can hire assistants to do this for you. In order to keep up with the self-publishing competition, you need to publish one Kindle eBook every six weeks (and that's the minimum). This entire process can take several months, but that's too long. By hiring assistants, you will be able to have someone else ask the questions for you and send you the paragraphs of content while you write the content for your Kindle eBook.

Summarizing Methods 13-25

No matter how many people visit your Kindle eBook's page, quality content is essential to boosting your sales. Writing about the ideal topic, solving a problem, and organizing your Kindle eBook properly with a table of contents will also make customers more likely to buy your Kindle eBook. After you are done writing your Kindle eBook, you need to proofread it and hire someone to design a good cover. As you get better at writing Kindle eBooks, you need to increase your frequency and write longer Kindle eBooks. When you increase your frequency and write longer Kindle eBooks, the math will make your dream of becoming a full-time self-published author easier to attain.

Methods 26-35: Utilizing Amazon's Tools And Optimizing Your Description

Amazon has a variety of tools and features that can help you get more sales for your Kindle eBooks. Many people know about these tools and features, but in order to get more sales, you need to optimize the tools and features that Amazon provides. In addition to tools and features, there are also certain elements of your Kindle eBook's description that have a big impact on how many sales they get.

Method #26: Use Kindle Countdown Deals

A Kindle countdown deal is a powerful way to boost your Kindle eBook sales. If your Kindle eBook is priced between $2.99 and $24.99, then you can use the Kindle Countdown Deals feature. This feature allows you to offer a discount for your Kindle eBook. Discounts are very powerful. If you have plenty of good reviews from customers who enjoyed reading your Kindle eBooks, potential customers will feel as if they are getting more than what they are paying for.

There are several successful self-published authors who use Kindle Countdown Deals and have reported that their sales doubled immediately after using Kindle Countdown Deals. These countdowns are especially good for your Kindle eBook titles that are old and not making as many sales. In addition to bringing your old titles back to life, you can run multiple Kindle Countdown Deals at the same time so you get some of your customers to buy multiple Kindle eBooks that you sell. This makes the three sales rule happen quicker. If three people buy three of your discounted Kindle eBooks, they are very likely to be customers for life. In addition, if your Kindle eBook is $2.99 or higher, and you lower that Kindle eBook's price to $0.99 with the Kindle Countdown Deal, you still make 70% of the sale. Instead of only making $0.35 per sale, you will be able to make $0.70 per sale. That does not sound like a big difference, but some Kindle Countdown Deals result in hundreds of extra sales. If your Kindle eBook makes 100 sales in 1 day from the Kindle Countdown Deal, that $70 now looks a lot better than $35.

Here's What Happens When The Countdown Expires

Within the countdown, more people buy your Kindle eBooks, and you will get some reviews as well. The countdown deals allow you to get the best reviewers for the lowest price because the naysayers tend to be the people who got the Kindle eBook for free. Amazon recognizes that your Kindle eBook made a lot of sales, and now Amazon starts promoting your Kindle eBook. As a result, you will get more sales from your Kindle eBook after the countdown expires. Although the sales you get from your Kindle eBook won't be as good as the countdown right when the price goes back to normal, you will see more sales for your Kindle eBooks after the countdown deal than what you were getting before the countdown deal.

The Only Problem About Kindle Countdown Deals

There are a lot of positives with Kindle Countdown Deals. The only problem with these deals is not the deals themselves. The problem is the process. No Kindle eBook can use Kindle Countdown Deals until 30 days after it got registered for KDP Select. That means if you want to use a Kindle Countdown Deal for a newly published Kindle eBook, that won't happen.

Since this limitation is in place, the best way to use Kindle Countdown Deals is by bringing life back to your old titles.

Getting People To Visit The Kindle Countdown Deal

In order to get people to visit your Kindle Countdown Deal, you need to tell people about the deal on your blog and social networks. Amazon promotes many Kindle Countdown Deals, and if Amazon chooses to promote your countdown deal, more people will be inclined to buy your Kindle eBook.

Why The Countdown Deal Works

The countdown deal is a powerful discount. Not only does it show the customer is getting more for his money, but customers also get to see how much time is left for the countdown. With time ticking away, the customer's decision making process becomes much shorter. Some people buy Kindle eBooks with Countdown Deals because customers want to avoid later regret when the Kindle eBook's price goes back to the original price. The countdown deal creates a powerful call to action that customers cannot ignore.

Method #27: Use The Free Promotion

The free promotion is a powerful way to boost your Kindle eBook sales. Although you will not make any money for that Kindle eBook for the days that you run the free promotion, more people will be able to know about your Kindle eBook. Your readership will grow, and some of those readers will buy your paid Kindle eBooks. One of the benefits of growing a readership is getting more reviews. Reviews don't come easy, and some of the bestselling Kindle eBooks that have been sold over 100,000 times only have 200 reviews to show for it. That means only 1 out of every 500 customers reviewed those books. Some people get reviews for their Kindle eBooks faster than others. It took me less than 10 paying customers to get a review for my book, *How To Be Successful On Twitter*.

My Experience With The Free Promotion

The first book that I did a free promotion for was *How To Publish More Kindle eBooks Faster*. I published the book in April 2014, and after hearing so many people say good things about the free promotion, I decided to give it a try. In the first day of the free promotion, my Kindle eBook was downloaded 171 times. My Kindle eBook became a #1 bestseller in two of the free categories, and on the next day, my Kindle eBook got sold 148 times. In addition, I got a 5 star review on that day. In the end, my Kindle eBook got downloaded over 500 times.

How A Free Book Affect Reviews
Offering a free Kindle eBook will definitely allow you to get more reviews. Although I have not been affected by this problem, many self-published authors mention that some people buy the book without reading the description. Then, these people leave 1 star reviews. The bad reviews are the only risk in offering your Kindle eBook for free, but overall, this is a strategy worth implementing. Offering a Kindle eBook for free will allow a new book to have a good launch or an old Kindle eBook to get more attention. In addition, once the free promotion expires, your Kindle eBook will start to make paid sales.

Factors That Contributed To Hundreds Of Downloads For My Kindle eBook
There were several factors that contributed to me getting hundreds of downloads for my Kindle eBook on the first try.
1. **Cool cover**. The cool cover was probably one of the biggest reasons why the Kindle eBook got downloaded hundreds of times. This was the first cover that I hired someone to create, and it paid off big time.
2. **The Kindle eBook's topic**. There are some (and in this case, some means over 1 million) people who want to make more money from their Kindle eBooks. One of the tactics to make more money from your Kindle eBooks is by publishing more Kindle eBooks faster. This was the kind of topic that many people want to know about which is another reason why the Kindle eBook got hundreds of downloads.

3. **I promoted my free Kindle eBook on my blog and social networks**. At the time, I had 69,000 followers and over 400 daily visitors for my blog. Many of the people who read the blog post bought the Kindle eBook, and I sent out periodic tweets about the Kindle eBook which also got attention.

This was the only mistake I made with my first free promotion:

Not having a marketing plan. Since it was my first time, I did not expect to need a marketing plan. As a result, I did not submit any of my Kindle eBooks to websites that would have been happy to promote them. However, the one mistake I made was a big one. Some people with marketing plans get as many as 6 downloads every minute. That is way better than something slightly over 500 within 5 days, but it was definitely a start. Before you make your Kindle eBook free, you must create a marketing plan for that Kindle eBook.

How To Create A Marketing Plan For Your Free Kindle eBook

Professional sports teams start every game with a plan. In order for you to become a successful self-published author, you need to start out with a plan as well. For you, this plan is the marketing plan. You need to come up with an effective marketing plan that results in an effective launch for your Kindle eBook. These are some of the things that you can include in your marketing plan:

1. **Telling 20-100 websites that your Kindle eBook will be free**. Tell these websites at least 1 month in advance so they know about you. In addition, you need to choose the right websites to promote your Kindle eBook on. Shelley Hitz did a good job sharing all of the places you can submit your free Kindle eBook to in her blog post, *76+ Places To Submit Your Free KDP Select Promotion For Your Kindle eBook*.

2. **The strategy you will use to get sales before the Kindle eBook goes free**. You need to get some sales before the free promotion starts to build your momentum. For the entire first month, you will have to promote your Kindle eBook on your own. The best ways to promote a Kindle eBook are with a blog and your social networks.

3. **Any other creative ideas you think of to market your Kindle eBook**. For this stage, there are no limits. Maybe you include a discount to a training course inside your Kindle eBook. Maybe you give a free PDF of your Kindle eBook to people who join your membership site. What creative versions of marketing will you think of?

The marketing plan is going to dictate what you need to do right when your Kindle eBook gets published. You don't want to be looking for ways to market your Kindle eBook after the launch. Then it's too late. You want to have the plan all figured out before you publish your Kindle eBook so you can easily promote it immediately when it gets published.

Method #28: Use Reddit To Get More Sales For A Free Promotion And Blog Traffic

Reddit is one of the easiest tools to use to go viral and get more people to know about your free promotion and your blog as well. Reddit can suddenly drive hundreds of extra people to your blog. There are many people who go viral on Reddit without knowing why, but once you master using Reddit, you will be able to go viral faster.

When To Post On Reddit

Based on a study of the Top 10,000 posts that went viral on Reddit, posting something on Reddit during the weekday boosts your chances of going viral although there is a slight advantage to post something on Reddit on a

Thursday. Regardless of which day of the week you post on Reddit, Saturdays and Sundays are no good for going viral. In addition, the timing of your post also impacts how likely it is to go viral. Any time between 9 am and 1 pm is a good time to publish a new post up on Reddit.

What Subreddits Are And Which Ones Get The Most Attention
Subreddits are categories that you label your posts under which allows people looking through those categories to find your posts. Out of all of the subreddits, funny is the most popular one of them all, but one of the subreddits you can use is videos. Videos is a very popular subreddit that gets a lot of attention. You can use the videos subreddit to promote a trailer for your book.

More Ways To Increase Your Chances Of Going Viral
The length of your title has a big impact on how likely your post is to go viral. Reddit posts that go viral have titles that are 30% longer than the average Reddit post. Use over 70 characters in your title to get the best results.

Method #29: Have Good Descriptions For Your Kindle eBooks

Having a good description for your Kindle eBooks is almost as important as writing quality Kindle eBooks. Your Kindle eBook's description is one of the deciding factors of whether someone will buy it or not. Few people know what makes a description for a Kindle eBook effective. The people who know how to write effective descriptions are the ones who are making thousands of dollars every month and in some cases over $100,000 every year. Effective descriptions have these characteristics:

1. **Brief summary**. Your description needs to contain a very brief summary of what gets discussed in your Kindle eBook. Remember that you are not giving everything away in your description. For a nonfiction Kindle eBook, you are highlighting 3-5 main things in that Kindle eBook. In a fiction Kindle eBook, you are giving a summary of the entire Kindle eBook so people get to know part of the story. Only knowing a part of the story will encourage more people to buy that Kindle eBook. Knowing nothing about those same Kindle eBooks will not encourage potential customers to buy them.

2. **Appeal to the customer's emotions**. An emotional description is one that gets a lot of sales. If you can tap into the customer's emotions, then that customer will be more inclined to buy a Kindle eBook from someone who understands what that customer is going through.

3. **Ask people to look inside your Kindle eBook and then download if it's right for them**. Few people ask their customers to look inside their Kindle eBooks and then download them if the first few pages looked good. Although this does add some pressure to make your first pages flawless, giving the customers a call to action makes them click "Look Inside." Maybe the next button they will press is the "Buy Now With 1 Click" button. When a customer reads your description, they are taking passive action. The customer is just reading what you wrote. Telling the customer to do something makes that customer active enough to fulfill the action you mentioned in your description. Some customers need to be given an action (clicking the "Buy Now" button) to fulfill before they will buy your Kindle eBook.

4. **Include reviews from notable people in your descriptions**. Ask notable, popular people to review your Kindle eBooks. Asking does not hurt. The worst thing that can happen is that some of these people say no. If you get someone from a popular newspaper, a bestselling author,

or someone else to review your Kindle eBook, then you can leave that review in your description. Leaving this review in your description will show potential customers that notable people read and enjoyed your Kindle eBook.

5. **Length**. The length of your description is also very important. You should write a long description because the people who read a long description are also more likely to buy your Kindle eBook. When you write the lengthy description, just be sure to combine the other 4 characteristics into that description.

Those are the five ways to write an effective description. The description is the pitch that gets the sale. Most people read the description before they decide whether or not to buy any product on Amazon let alone a Kindle eBook. The more phenomenal your description is, the more downloads your Kindle eBook is going to get.

Method #30: Make Sure Your Kindle eBook's Message Is Clear

One of the most important ways to get more sales is by making sure your Kindle eBook's message is clear. Your Kindle eBook's title, subtitle, cover, and description all need to support each other so your customer knows exactly what it is about. If your customers have no idea what your Kindle eBook is about, then they will not buy it. It is very important to remember that confused customers never buy. Even if you wrote a Kindle eBook better than anyone else in your niche, no one will buy it if the title, subtitle, cover, or description do not make any sense.

Be Specific

The best way to make your Kindle eBook clear is by being as specific as possible. The more specific you are, the narrower your targeted audience becomes. That may sound like a bad thing, but a "narrowed down" targeted audience in most cases still means over 1 million people. Being specific will also make the narrowed down targeted audience more likely to buy your Kindle eBook since it solves more specific problems.

Method #31: Ask For The Sale

Every self-published author wants to make the first sale, and then the desire to make more sales grows. The customer is well aware that you want him to buy your Kindle eBook. Why not ask the customer to buy your Kindle eBook instead of leaving it up to chance? There is no harm in asking, and some of the most successful self-published authors ask all of their potential customers to look at their Kindle eBook with the free previewer while other successful self-published authors even go a step further by asking their customers to click the Buy Now button. What successful people have in common is that they "ask their way to success."

Method #32: Turn Your Kindle eBook Into A Physical Book

There are plenty of benefits to creating a physical edition of your Kindle eBook. The benefit many authors think about is the bragging rights. Bragging rights can range from showing friends your physical books to signing your own physical books after people buy them. In addition to bragging rights, there are plenty of other benefits of publishing a physical book as well.

No matter how much you try to inform customers, there will still be some people who visit your Kindle eBook's Amazon page and believe that they must have a Kindle device in order to read your content. Having a physical version of the same Kindle eBook solves the problem. Physical books remove the limitation of having a Kindle device, a Kindle app, or Cloud

Reader on your computer. While Kindle eBooks are priced more conveniently, some people prefer to read physical books. By giving your customers both options, you will increase the likelihood of making the sale.

How Physical Books Become Very Important When You Do Public Speaking

As you become a more established expert in your niche, some people may contact you with speaking opportunities. While these speaking opportunities are great ways to get more people to know about you, you must have something for customers to buy at the speaking event. If you do a wonderful job as a public speaker, people will want to buy your books right away. If you tell these people that your books are only available on Kindle, there is a big time lapse that may result in you losing a customer who was eager to buy one of your books when they saw you in person. Strike while the iron is hot.

As more time goes by after you did your speech, the people who heard your speech will be less likely to buy your books on their Kindle devices or apps. The people you talked to could have become returning customers, but since the connection got broken, it never happened. This is the problem that results from only having Kindle eBooks available. A physical book solves this problem. People can buy your physical book minutes after they heard you speak, and it is at this time when most of the audience will be eager to buy from you. While sales can be completed online, there is nothing like real human interaction. People who see you and get to talk to you will be more likely to buy your physical books before leaving the event. In June 2013, I did not know anything about Mike Michalowicz. When I saw him perform as a public speaker that summer, I immediately learned about Michalowicz's story. In addition, I bought his physical book, *The Pumpkin Plan*, right after his presentation was over. After I bought the physical book, he signed it.

The Power Of A Book Signing

One of the easiest ways to get a returning customer is to sign their copy of your physical book. Mike Michalowicz and Seth Godin are two authors who signed my copies of their physical books. Since then, I have bought several of these authors' physical books and read them all. I reference these authors in multiple blog posts and some of my Kindle eBooks as well. I am also subscribed to their blogs and watch videos and podcasts that feature them.

A book signing allows you to have a short connection with the customer where you give that customer your undivided attention. This short connection becomes stronger for those people as the days go by. This short connection is what results in people becoming returning customers. The best part is that it only takes a presentation and a signature to create a strong connection in a short amount of time.

Method #33: Create An Effective Author Page

Amazon gives you the ability to create an Author Page. On this page, you are able to display all of the Kindle eBooks that you have written. It is very easy for you to create an Author Central Page for yourself. All you need to do is go to www.authorcentral.amazon.com and create an account. Once you get to the dashboard, go to books and click on "Add more books" to display your latest books. The Author Central Page makes it much easier for returning customers to find your content. In addition, your potential customers may see one of your Kindle eBooks but want a Kindle eBook on a different topic related to your niche. If the Kindle eBook your potential customer is looking at is about Twitter, and they want a Kindle eBook on Pinterest, then the Kindle eBook about Twitter is not the answer. However, if you already wrote a Kindle eBook about Pinterest, and the potential customers visits your Author Central Page, that potential customer will see your Kindle eBook about Pinterest and buy it. The Author Central Page allows you to emphasize the diversity of your product range.

The Components Of An Effective Author Page

Not all author pages are created equal. Out of all of the components of an effective sales page, your bio is the most important part. The ideal bio should consist of at least three paragraphs and discuss the following:

1. **The types of Kindle eBooks you publish**. This allows your potential customer to decide whether your Kindle eBooks are the right ones for him or not.

2. **How frequently you publish new Kindle eBooks**. If you tell your customers that you publish one Kindle eBook every month (and if you go by that promise), your customers will be visiting your author page every month to buy your next Kindle eBook. In addition, if a customer does not like any of the Kindle eBooks you have, there's always next month (not next year) for a Kindle eBook to come out that the particular customer will like. You have 12 chances every year to impress a potential customer enough to buy one of your Kindle eBooks. That's enough chances to ensure a sale assuming that you write great content and your potential customer is targeted.

3. **Your accomplishments and milestones**. People don't buy from anyone. You need to be qualified for the sale. Telling people about your accomplishments and milestones that you have reached will encourage people to buy your Kindle eBooks. Some of my accomplishments include winning the Rule Breaker's Award, teaching entrepreneurship at Fordham University while attending high school, and being a teenager author. Do not be afraid to toot your own horn in your bio.

4. **Something that makes you stand out**. All of the big-time self-published authors have a list of accomplishments and publish Kindle eBooks often. However, each self-published author stands out for a particular reason. I

stand out because I have the fearlessness of a teenager and the dedication of an entrepreneur. Why do you stand out? Let your customers know.

Although the bio is the most important component of your author page, there are other components that are very important. Displaying your Twitter account and blog are important as well. Your Twitter account gives your potential customers an idea of how influential you are on the web. If you have 100,000 Twitter followers, then potential customers will be more likely to buy your products. In addition, potential customers can directly contact you on Twitter, and if you give them a warm reply, that potential customer will feel more confident about their decision to buy your Kindle eBook. Providing a link to your blog gives your potential customers an idea of the value of your Kindle eBook's content. If your blog posts are valuable, then your potential customers will believe that your Kindle eBooks are also valuable. This works vice-versa, so although it is important to focus on your Kindle eBooks, it is also important to make sure your free content is really good. Really good free content means super good paid content.

There is no author page complete without a photo of yourself. Make sure the photo of yourself looks professional and is clear. A blurry photo does not go well with potential customers. Having the picture of yourself builds the trust that your potential customers look for before making a purchase.

Method #34: Optimize Your Keywords

Since Amazon is the 4th largest search engines on the web, keywords are very important for getting more exposure on Amazon. However, this is the part of selling that few people know well. Optimizing your keywords in your title, subtitle, and description will allow your Kindle eBook to get found for various searches.

How To Find The Right Keywords For You

You can only have seven keywords for your book. Choosing popular keywords will help you out in the long run if your book ends up being #1 for that keyword, but if your Kindle eBook does not get a lot of sales, then it will remain hidden by the other books with the same popular keyword. However, if you choose a keyword phrase that few people would search for on Amazon, then no one will know about your Kindle eBook..

When it comes to the length of a Kindle eBook's keywords, some people make their keywords too long. If your keyword phrase is more than seven words long, chances are few people are going to search it. However, some two word keyword phrases are too crowded, and only the bestselling Kindle eBooks show up on top for those kinds of keywords. Luckily, there is a free tool, the Google Adwords Keyword Lookup Tool, that allows you to find other popular keywords options on Amazon related to any keyword in your niche. This keyword tool is based on data from Google Adwords, but since both Google and Amazon are popular search engines, they are getting visitors who are searching for the same information. You can use the Google Adwords Keyword Lookup Tool to see which keywords are popular (the keywords you want to have), the ones that have medium popularity (you should have two keywords in this category so it is easier for people to find your book when they search your category), and the ones that have low popularity (the ones you need to avoid). By choosing the best keywords for your Kindle eBook, you will put yourself in a position to make more long-term sales.

What You Need To Do After Choosing Your Keywords

After choosing your keywords, you need to add some of those keywords into the title and subtitle of your Kindle eBook. While you can only pick and choose for this part, all of the keywords you choose need to be in your description. It is very easy to write a compelling description that uses all of the keywords. Let's say your three keywords are Twitter followers, Twitter engagement, and Twitter book. You can mention all three of these keywords in your description's first three sentences like this:

"Do you want more Twitter followers? Do you want to boost your Twitter engagement? If you want to grow your presence on Twitter, this Twitter Kindle eBook is the right one for you..."

Here's another example:

"In this Twitter Kindle eBook, you will learn how to get more Twitter followers and boost your Twitter engagement so you can build long lasting connections with the people in your audience..."

There are numerous ways to craft your description so it has all of the keywords. The more keywords your Kindle eBook has, the easier it will be for people to find that book on Amazon's search engine.

Method #35: Label Your Kindle eBook With The Right Categories

The categories you choose for your Kindle eBooks are essential towards getting more sales. Not only do you need to choose three categories, but you need to choose the right categories for your Kindle eBook. Most of the Kindle eBooks that landed in the Top 100 Bestsellers List on all of Amazon is because those Kindle eBooks reached the Top 10 in their categories first. Reaching the Top 100 in any category will allow your Kindle eBook to get more sales. When my Kindle eBook *How To Publish More Kindle eBooks Faster* reached the Top 100 for multiple categories, it immediately went from getting 1 sale every two days to getting 2 sales every day. As the book got closer to #1 status, it got more sales.

If you get into the Top 100 bestsellers list for one of your categories and stay there for a while, that Kindle eBook will eventually become a Top 100 bestseller in all of the categories you choose for that Kindle eBook. The more Top 100 bestsellers lists your Kindle eBook appears on, the more Amazon promotes it on their site. In order to get to the Top 100 bestsellers list in any category (and stay there), you need to choose the right categories for your Kindle eBook. By choosing the right categories for your Kindle eBook, the customers who look at your Kindle eBook in its category will have a desire to buy it. No matter how big or small that desire is for the customer to buy your Kindle eBook, that desire will grow over time as they see your Kindle eBook more often. Some customers may buy your Kindle eBook after seeing it seven times on Amazon's site. Others take longer, but in the end, you make the sale.

How To Find The Right Categories For Your Kindle eBooks

KDP does a great job at providing a lot of categories, but with so many categories to choose from, finding the ideal categories for your Kindle eBook is not as easy as it sounds. It may take you 10 minutes just to browse through all of KDP's category options and then another five minutes to decide which categories are the right ones for your Kindle eBook.

Of course, there is another approach. Chances are there are people in your niche who have written similar Kindle eBooks. There are dozens of other Kindle eBooks about getting more Kindle sales, being successful on Twitter, and writing more words every day. Instead of looking through KDP's list of categories and deciding which categories properly identify your Kindle eBooks, look at the categories that other authors chose. There is no reason to do extra, unnecessary work that someone else has already done for you. This will save you a lot of time while ensuring that you are making the right decision for your Kindle eBook.

One More Thing

While it is important to choose the categories that your Kindle eBook fits, it is also important to choose the categories that are easy to end up on the Top 100 Bestsellers Page. All you need to do is go to each category and see the Kindle overall rank for Kindle eBooks ranked 80-100 on the list. The higher those ranks are, the easier it will be for your Kindle eBook to land on one of those Top 100 Bestsellers Pages. My recommendation is to still go with the categories that your competitors chose, but if you are considering three categories but can only choose two, this is a great way to decide which categories are the best ones for your Kindle eBook.

Summarizing Methods 26-35

Having access to the same tools and features that millions of other self-published authors have access to does not give you an advantage. Instead, utilizing those tools differently so you get better results will give you a distinct advantage in the competition. In addition to utilizing these tools and features effectively, your Kindle eBook's description has a big impact on how many sales it gets. Your description (and your Kindle eBook) needs to have a clear message and ask the person to read some of your Kindle eBook with the free previewer and eventually click the "Buy with 1 click button." How you utilize Amazon's tools and features will result in the most traffic to your Kindle eBooks. The descriptions will decide how many people buy your Kindle eBooks.

Methods 36-44: Prelaunch, Launch, And Getting Reviews

Your Kindle eBook's prelaunch and launch are two of the most important stages of your Kindle eBook. The more sales your Kindle eBooks generate during the launch, the better it will rank in the Kindle store. The prelaunch helps you build awareness of your Kindle eBook and get eager customers waiting for the release date. One of the important things you need to do during your Kindle eBook's launch is get reviews. A Kindle eBook with 10 good reviews is going to get sold more often than a Kindle eBook with only 1 good review. As you get more reviews, you will also have the ability to showcase those positive reviews to potential customers who are thinking of buying your Kindle eBook.

Method #36: Have A Good Prelaunch

Having a good prelaunch for your Kindle eBook is critical towards its success. The goal of a prelaunch is to get as many people are possible to know about your Kindle eBook before it gets published. As you build a following and tell them about your Kindle eBook, people will be eager to read your next Kindle eBook. As a result, you will be able to build stronger connections with the people who are emailing you every week to ask when your Kindle eBook comes out. If multiple people are asking you about when your Kindle eBook comes out, then you know your prelaunch was very effective.

How To Create The Buzz The Right Way

The best way to create an effective prelaunch is by creating the buzz for your Kindle eBook. Simply telling everyone that you will be publishing a Kindle eBook in a few months is not an effective way to create the buzz. Instead, you need to tell the people who will want to buy your Kindle eBook. If you have built a targeted following around Facebook marketing tips, your followers would be more eager to buy a Kindle eBook about Facebook marketing than a Kindle eBook about Pinterest marketing.

Not everyone will pay attention to the buzz you create for your Kindle eBooks. Some people will not care about your Kindle eBooks' topics, and no matter how much you try, these people will not become a part of your audience. Instead, share the buzz with targeted people who would like to become a part of your target audience. These people are more likely to spread the buzz you created and help keep that buzz alive.

If you want people to create a strong buzz for your Kindle eBook, get a team of 10 people to promote your Kindle eBook to their social media audiences, blogs related to your Kindle eBook, and similar places. Depending on your legacy, you may be able to get some of these people to work on no pay. Some people would be happy to do the job just for promotion. If your Kindle eBook becomes a bestseller, you can promise a 1 week vacation somewhere with you and all of the members of your team. There are countless ways to create the buzz for your product, but being creative as you create the buzz for your product is essential.

Create Book Trailers On YouTube

A very creative way to add buzz to your Kindle eBooks is by uploading book trailers on YouTube. Book trailers on YouTube are powerful. Mike Michalowicz used book trailers to promote his book, *The Pumpkin Plan*, and his videos ended up generating over 100,000 views, and the book became a bestseller. Book trailers will allow all of your subscribers to know about your upcoming Kindle eBooks.

Method #37: Be Able To Make 50 Sales On Launch Day

The presence you have on the web is an important factor that decides how many sales you get. Methods 1-12 showed you how to grow a bigger presence on the web. The launch is a pivotal factor that determines how long it will take for your book to become successful. Implementing Methods 1-12 at a consistent, frequent rate will make 50 sales easier to reach on launch day.

Why 50 Sales?

To be quite honest, 50 is the minimum. If you happen to make 100 sales on launch day, that's even better. However, 50 sales is the number you need to reach so your Kindle eBook gets a strong rank on Amazon's bestsellers list. A big factor that goes in towards your Kindle eBook's ranking on Amazon is how many sales that Kindle eBook is able to make within 24-36 hours. If your Kindle eBook makes 50 sales within that time period, then it will go on the Top 100 lists for multiple categories.

As your Kindle eBook continues to appear on more Top 100 lists, more people will buy them on Amazon. Even if these people never heard about your blog or don't follow you on any of your social networks, these people will still buy your Kindle eBook because Amazon is now promoting it more often. In addition, when you make more sales, your Kindle eBook will get a better rank on bestsellers lists. The #1 bestselling Kindle eBook in any category gets seen more often than the Kindle eBook that is the #100 bestseller in the same category.

For some categories, you only need to make 1 sale every day in order to get on and stay on a bestsellers list. By getting 50 sales on launch day, Amazon will promote your Kindle eBook more often, and soon you will see that title making a consistent and very good amount of sales every day.

Method #38: Get More Reviews

Getting more reviews is one of the most important ways to get more sales. A large quantity of good reviews will make potential customers realize that there are a lot of people who read and enjoyed your Kindle eBook's content. The positive reviews will encourage a customer to buy your Kindle eBook.

One way to get more reviews is by offering your Kindle eBook for free. Offering your Kindle eBook for free will result in a high volume of sales. Some of the people who bought your Kindle eBook will also be encouraged to review it. Although many self-published authors have reported getting most of their 1 star reviews for offering their Kindle eBooks for free, I have not encountered this problem yet. Ultimately, by offering your Kindle eBook for free for 5 days will allow you to see a rise in paid sales immediately after that Kindle eBook is no longer free.

Another great way to get more reviews is by using the Kindle Countdown Deal. Although you may not get as many downloads for the Countdown Deal compared to the free promotion, the people who buy Kindle eBooks for a lower price tend to leave better reviews than the people who download Kindle eBooks for free. You can only start to use a Kindle Countdown Deal 30 days after your Kindle eBook has been enrolled to the KDP Select Program.

Ultimately, the best way to get reviews for your Kindle eBook is by spreading the word. You want as many people as possible to buy your Kindle eBooks so they leave reviews. If you have a big list, and you tell everyone on that list about your Kindle eBook, some of those people will be very likely to review it. You can also ask friends to review the Kindle eBook you just published. The possibilities for getting more reviews for your Kindle eBooks are endless.

How Important Are Reviews

Reviews are super important for your Kindle eBooks. The bestselling Kindle eBooks happen to have well over 100 reviews. That's not a coincidence. Customers are looking at reviews more than ever, and reviews have a big impact on whether a customer buys a product or not. These are some of the statistics about reviews and their impact on customers.

1. 62% of customers read consumer-written product reviews online.
2. 80% say their purchase decisions have been directly influenced by reviews.
3. 70% of shoppers share product reviews with their friends, family, or colleagues.

Those are some big percentages. Reviews have a powerful impact on how many sales your Kindle eBooks get. The more reviews your book has, the better.

An Easy Way To Get Five Star Reviews

If you want to get more five star reviews, leave a "Thank You" at the end of your Kindle eBook thanking the customer for choosing you instead of the dozens of competitors. At the end of your "Thank You," tell the customer that if they learned something from your Kindle eBook, you would be grateful if that person could leave a review.

Not only are you getting more 5 star reviews, but you are also discouraging people who didn't like your Kindle eBook to leave 1 star reviews. No matter how good your Kindle eBook is, there will be a person who does not like it. This part of the Thank You note discourages those people from leaving bad reviews which will ultimately keep the average number of stars high.

Method #39: Thank The People Who Wrote Good Reviews

The people who wrote good reviews liked the content in your Kindle eBook. A great way to show how appreciative you are of your customer's good review is by thanking the customer for reviewing your Kindle eBook. Thanking that customer tells that customer that he is important, and that customer will buy your other Kindle eBooks and continue to leave good reviews.

Readers who enjoy reading an author's Kindle eBook love getting contacted by surprise from that author. Contacting these readers allows you to give them the surprise they were not expecting. That surprise is what allows you to build strong connections with your readers, and as a result, more returning customers.

How To Contact People Who Wrote A Good Review

Sadly, it is not possible to contact everyone who writes a good review for your Kindle eBook. The only way to properly thank someone for reviewing your Kindle eBook is if they included their website in their bio. Without the website, you will not be able to contact the reviewer. However, if you are able to contact the reviewer, thank that reviewer as soon as possible. The sooner you thank the reviewer, the more grateful that person will be when you thank them.

What To Say In The Thank You To The Reviewer

The Thank You's that are short and sweet are the ones that work the best. For this email, take out all of the links to your social networks and Kindle eBooks. Only include a link to your blog directly below the signature. Here is a rubric email that you can use:

Dear _____,

I saw that you recently left a review for my Kindle eBook, _____. I just wanted to stop by and thank you for reviewing it. I love getting feedback about my content so I can identify whether the content I write gives my readers the best experience or not. I am very appreciative of your honest feedback and look forward to staying in touch.

Regards,
Marc Guberti
www.marcguberti.com

That's all it takes. Your readers are very busy people, and you want your Thank You to be as brief as possible. In just four sentences, I am able to relay the message. I could have written a Thank You in four paragraphs, but that would take too long for someone to read. Since your message will most likely appear in someone's inbox, you want to give your reader the ability to read your message quickly for two reasons:

1. **Your message is not the only one in their inbox**. Some of the messages people receive are spam that get thrown in the trash, subscriptions to blogs on the web, or clients contacting them. To quickly sum it all up, your message is not the only one in their inbox. If your Thank You message is four sentences, the person is more likely to read your entire message. If your Thank You message is four paragraphs long, the person will be more likely to either skim through what you wrote or ignore the email.

2. **People are more likely to reply to your message**. When people get a short message, they tend to leave a short reply, but when people get a long message, they tend to leave a long reply. The shorter reply takes

less time to create than the longer reply. You want your readers to be able to reply to you as quickly as possible. Writing a short message will make the reader more likely to reply faster.

Shorter emails are simpler for people to read. Twitter was able to become a successful social network because of its simplicity. If you want to build strong connections with the people who left you good reviews, then you need to make it as simple as possible for these people to read the email.

Do Not Get In Touch With The People Who Gave You A Bad Review
Many self-published authors are tempted to get in touch with the people who left bad reviews. These people think that getting in touch with the person who left the bad review will lighten the mood, and the person who sent out the bad review might change his mind about your Kindle eBook. Contacting these people wastes time, and in the end, the problem almost never gets resolved. Contacting the person who left you a bad review may only make the problem worse.

Think of it from your standpoint. Let's say you gave a Kindle eBook a 1 star review because it was filled with typos, bad sentences, and methods that didn't even work. If the author contacted you asking for forgiveness and seeing whether you could change your review or not, you would probably not be very happy about that. Not only is this someone whose content you didn't like, but now this person is trying to get you to like their content. Your opinion about a Kindle eBook will probably not change just because the author contacted you.

Instead of contacting the people who left you bad reviews, only contact the people who left good reviews and thank them for leaving the review. Most popular people do not bother talking to the people who criticize them. Instead, these people talk to those who support their efforts. Instead of trying to get the critics to care about what you do, talk to the people who already care about what you do.

Method #40: Build Strong Connections With The Customers Who Buy Your Kindle eBook

When a customer buys your Kindle eBook, you need to get in touch with that customer. By building strong connections with the people who have already bought one of your Kindle eBooks, you will make these people more likely to become returning customers.

The problem that KDP presents is that although it has done a better job at tracking sales over the years, KDP does not allow you to access customer information. This makes the customer feel more confident about the order because his personal information is being protected. However, as the author, thanking each customer for buying your Kindle eBook is a difficult process. In some cases, authors have no idea who bought their Kindle eBooks until the customer decides to leave a review. Since a low percentage of your customers will leave reviews, waiting for customers to leave reviews before contacting them will only allow you to talk to a small percentage of your customers.

Unless the rules change dramatically, you will never be able to start a conversation with a customer who bought your Kindle eBook and does not follow you on any social network. The best option for having more conversations with your customers is by including your email address at the very end of your Kindle eBook. Just in case you were curious, my email address is marcguberti@optonline.net. Including your email address gives your customer the option to contact you. Since you are allowing customers to choose whether they want to contact you or not, most of the people who contact you will be the customers who enjoyed reading your Kindle eBook. By having long conversations with the customers who bought one of your Kindle eBooks for the first time, those customers will be very likely to buy your other Kindle eBooks as well. All you need to do at this point is get two more sales, and then the customer is a customer for life.

How To Properly Introduce Your Email Address

If you want people to contact you, these people need to have a reason to contact you. Simply telling people your email address will not result in more people contacting you (unless you're one of the celebrities with over 1 million Twitter followers). You should be able to explain in a short paragraph why people would want to contact you. These are some things you can say in that paragraph so people will want to connect with you:

1. **What you can talk about**. You can contact me for any other Kindle advice. By telling people what they can contact you about, you are further strengthening your status as an expert in your niche. If you provide the customer with what he is looking for, then that customer will be more likely to buy one of your other Kindle eBooks as well.

2. **Just to say hi**. Include this at the end of your paragraph. Although this is the last reason why people would want to contact you, adding this to your paragraph will get the wheels turning. Then, some people will contact you just to say hi, and the conversation will develop.

3. **Include your signature after the paragraph**. All you need to do is say something like, "I look forward to your success" and then have your name directly below. This will make the customer feel good because you care for them and want them to be successful. Including this ending will make the customer feel more inclined to contact you. If you include this signature at the end of the paragraph, that signature needs to be your sentiment. Don't write "I look forward to your success" just because I told you to write it. If you write "I look forward to your success," then that needs to be your sentiment. I look forward to your success because I am excited to see you turn your self-published Kindle eBooks into a full-time income just like I did. I want to see your Kindle eBooks thrive and be

successful. If you write "I look forward to your success," then you have to mean it.

By adding these three parts to your paragraph when you reveal your email address, customers will be more likely to contact you. Making the customer feel warm inside will make that customer trust you. This trust may result in that customer sending you an email, subscribing to your blog, and eventually buying one of your products.

Method #41: Add Reviews Of Your Kindle eBook To Your Blog And That Kindle eBook's Description

According to Neil Patel from QuickSprout, research is one of the four stages of getting a customer to buy your Kindle eBook for the first time. If a potential customer is already doing research, that means the person is aware about your product (the first stage). After doing the research, that potential customer will do a final search for information to confirm this is the Kindle eBook they want to buy and then make a purchase. Right when the person finds your Kindle eBook, you want to make the researching and final search parts of the sale easier for your potential customer. The best way to do that is by including some of the good things that people have already said about your Kindle eBook in its description and on your blog. This gives your potential customers the information that they are looking for: what people have already said about your Kindle eBook. For some potential customers, the reviews you include in your description may be all of the researching and final searching that they need to decide that your Kindle eBook is the right Kindle eBook for them.

How To Get A Well-Known Person To Review Your Book

When you include reviews in your Kindle eBook's description and on your blog, the reviews would be more powerful if potential customers already knew the people who reviewed your Kindle eBook. Potential customers won't know anything about a random friend, but names like Seth Godin and Mike Michalowicz sound familiar. Some people buy Kindle eBooks just because a famous person that they know left a review for that Kindle eBook.

In order to get a well-known person to review your Kindle eBook, you need to send them a free physical edition for your Kindle eBook and make sure that your Kindle eBook matches the person's interests. If the famous person you want to get in touch with is a social media expert, only send that person your physical book if it is about social media. When these people say yes to your request, send them the physical book for free. Receiving your physical book for free will encourage these people to leave a good review. If you want to boost your chances of getting a 5 star review from these people, sign your physical book and include a surprise book as an extra gift. Then, when these people review your book, you will be able to display that review in its description and on your blog. Getting this review will add to your credibility and make more people recognize your Kindle eBooks as products packed with quality content.

Method #42: Have A Sales Page For Your Kindle eBook

A common mistake that many authors make is leading people straight from their blog to the Kindle eBook's product page on Amazon. I was one of the many people who made this mistake. The common trend was for me to get hundreds of clicks but only a few sales. For some months, my conversion rate was lower than 1% which is really bad.

Looking back at my experiences of getting more conversion, I remembered a time when one of my Kindle eBook averaged 1-2 sales every day. At the time, that was a big milestone for me. The main reason I got that many sales every day was because that particular Kindle eBook had its own sales page. Once the sales page for that Kindle eBook got less traffic, the Kindle eBook also got less sales.

If you immediately send the person over to Amazon, you do not have a lot of time to build someone's desire to buy your Kindle eBook. Someone who has not read any of your Kindle eBooks does not have a strong desire to buy any of them. In order to give them a strong desire to buy your Kindle eBooks, you need to build that desire with a sales page for your Kindle eBooks.

8 Components That Make Up An Effective Sales Page

Amazon has a character limit for the description. However, if you are writing a sales page on your blog or on your own hub (I use Squidoo), you have no character limit. You can write as many characters as you want. My recommendation is to write a large amount of content in your sales page. Without any further adieu, here are the components that make up an effective sales page for your Kindle eBook:

1. **Have a video of you and physical book**. Having a physical book will tell people that your Kindle eBook is good enough to become a physical book. CreateSpace allows anyone to create physical books, and potential customers will see your physical book as a sign that your Kindle eBook is better than the average Kindle eBook. In addition, people would enjoy having the option of watching your video to learn more about your product.

2. **Have a giant sales page**. Having a decent sized sales page is not enough. Your sales page needs to be humongous. If your sales page is shorter than 2,000 words and only has 2 pictures, then it's too short. Your sales page needs to be something that takes at least five minutes for someone to read. A 2,000 word sales page will take anyone at least five minutes to read.

3. **Make your Kindle eBook irresistible**. The only way people will buy your Kindle eBook is if you explain your Kindle eBook in a way that makes it irresistible. The irresistible products are the ones that get sold the most. If you are writing a nonfiction Kindle eBook, you would make it irresistible by promising the reader that certain things will be in your Kindle eBook. One of the promises for this book was that it would provide you with 77 methods you can use to get more Kindle eBook sales. If you are going to write a fiction Kindle eBook, tell people about the adventure. What happens in your fiction Kindle eBook? Better yet, what happens in your fiction Kindle eBook that separates it from the other fiction Kindle eBooks available on the Kindle?

4. **Have a "Buy Now" button at three locations throughout the sales page**. Most people will skim through your sales page. Some people may not reach the bottom of your sales page before they decide that they want to buy your Kindle eBook. The only problem is that some people change their mind about buying a Kindle eBook as they scroll down to the bottom of the sales page. Some people will get agitated if they want to buy the Kindle eBook but have to scroll all the way down to see the "Buy Now" button. In addition, people who are not fully convinced the first time they see the "Buy Now" button are more likely to get convinced as they see the "Buy Now" button more often. It is important to remember that trust comes from being seen frequently. You have your best friend who you trust more than other friends because you see that best friend often. By showing customers the "Buy Now" button three times, their trust in your Kindle eBook will grow, and they will eventually buy it.

5. **Include testimonials about your Kindle eBook on your sales page**. Testimonials are an essential part of your sales page. 80% of customers get directly influenced by testimonials when making a purchase. If you

have good testimonials of your Kindle eBook on your sales page, people will be more likely to buy it. Not only do potential customers buy into your Kindle eBook, but they also buy into the testimonials. A problem with testimonials on a sales page is that many potential customers are quick to assume that these testimonials are from fake people. When there are no testimonials for their product, many people fake testimonials and use made up names. Instead of doing that, you need to include links to these people's websites to prove that they are real. If you do not have a link to a reviewer's website, use that person's social network. If you do not have any testimonials yet, ask some of your friends to leave good reviews for your Kindle eBook on Amazon. Then, use those reviews of your Kindle eBook as testimonials. My advice is to have at least 3 testimonials but no more than 9 testimonials on your sales page.

6. **Use pictures that people would want to see**. When you create your sales page, it is important to use pictures that would entice people to buy your Kindle eBook. If your nonfiction Kindle eBook is about getting more sales, potential customers would want to see your income reports. If your Kindle eBook is about running faster, people will want to see a picture of you in front of everyone else. If your Kindle eBook is about creating toys out of wood, people will want to see pictures of you with wooden toys that you made. For fiction Kindle eBooks, people will want to see pictures of scenes depicted in that Kindle eBook. When you choose which pictures go on your sales page, only be sure to choose from your Kindle eBook's best scenes or your best work.

7. **Add qualifications for your Kindle eBook**. No matter what your Kindle eBook is about, it isn't for everyone. Some customers need to be ensured that they are making the right decision. Mentioning who your Kindle eBook is for will ensure a customer that he is making the right decision. Not all of the 6 billion people on the planet are a part of your target audience. An example of this would be the qualifications for a

Kindle eBook about running faster being the following: You like to run, you want to run faster, you run for at least an hour every day, and you want to win in races. These qualifications will allow your customers to get a good picture of whether your Kindle eBook is right for them or not. In most cases, these qualifications will only make your potential customers want to buy your Kindle eBook more.

8. **Include your signature at the end of your sales page**. It is easy for a customer to forget that the Kindle eBook on the sales page was written by a human. By including your signature at the end of your sales page, you will remind everyone that someone wrote the Kindle eBook--you. Including your signature at the very end is the icing on the cake that makes potential customers realize that you care for their success, well-being, or their entertainment. The signature must end the sales page. No "Buy Now" button or paragraph can be placed below your signature.

Those are the 8 components that make up a good sales page. By utilizing these components, you will increase the chances of create a sales page that makes your Kindle eBook irresistible. The people who buy your Kindle eBook through the sales page are more likely to become customers for life. In addition, those customers are more likely to leave a positive review for your Kindle eBook. As you get more reviews for your Kindle eBook, you will be able to add more testimonials to your sales page. Getting more reviews will make your Kindle eBook look more attractive to potential customers who look at it on Amazon before looking anywhere else.

You may now be starting to realize that all of these methods are connected. Many of these methods support each other, and all of these methods have the common goal of increasing your Kindle eBook sales. That is a good thing to know.

Method #43: Don't Abandon Your Kindle eBook After It Gets Launched

The single biggest mistake I have seen self-published authors make is abandoning their Kindle eBooks right after the launch. After that, self-published authors expect the Kindle eBooks to sell themselves without their involvement. These people want to create systematized products so they can get more sales and write more Kindle eBooks without worrying about the old ones.

The problem is that as Kindle eBooks get older, there are more customers who already bought that Kindle eBook. In addition, most of the newer Kindle eBooks look more enticing than the older ones. If you saw two Kindle eBooks about Facebook marketing that had the same number of pages, but the only thing different was the publication date, chances are you would choose to buy the book that got published earlier. A Kindle eBook about Facebook marketing that was published in 2006 is not going to get as many sales right now as a Kindle eBook about Facebook marketing that was published in 2012.

It Is Entirely Okay To Update Your Kindle eBook

In fact, updating your book will lead to more returning customers. Seth Godin updated his book *Purple Cow* with numerous case studies. The case studies further strengthened the message of *Purple Cow* and resulted in more readers coming back to buy the updated book. It is important to update your Kindle eBook because some of the information in your Kindle eBook may get outdated. There are now more Facebook marketing tactics than there were in 2006. In 2006, Facebook Advertising was not nearly as big as it is today. Instagram wasn't even part of the picture in 2006. Things change, and in order to get more sales for your Kindle eBooks in the long-term, they should reflect upon those changes. If you want to preserve your old Kindle eBook, you can write a Part 2 so customers can buy the new Kindle eBook while having an idea of what your old Kindle eBook provided. The new Kindle eBook will also encourage sales for the older one because there will be people who wonder what Facebook marketing was like in 2006.

For The Self-Published Authors With Evergreen Content
The Kindle eBooks with evergreen content never get old. Someone can be reading your Kindle eBook several years later, and the content will still make sense. Although a Kindle eBook about Facebook marketing published in 2006 needs a revision, evergreen content does not need to be revised after publication. However, it is still important to market your evergreen Kindle eBooks after they get launched. You cannot assume that just because you wrote evergreen content that people will come, buy it, and the process will repeat from generation to generation. In order to make that happen, you need to continue promoting your Kindle eBook. Run another free promotion for your Kindle eBook, have another Kindle Countdown deal, and promote your Kindle eBook in another one of your blog posts.

Your Kindle eBook Sales Will Gradually Decline Unless You Take A Stand
Your Kindle eBook may be on the Top 100 bestsellers lists for multiple categories. However, there will eventually come a time when newer Kindle eBooks bump what you wrote further down on those lists. If you do not continue to market your Kindle eBook, then the newer Kindle eBooks will eventually bump your Kindle eBook off of the Top 100 bestsellers lists for all of its categories. You do not want to see all of your hard work and dedication result in something as catastrophic as that. As you see a decline in any individual Kindle eBook's sales, you need to make that

Kindle eBook the irresistible product that people want yet again. The Kindle Countdown Deal is a huge factor because it keeps your Kindle eBook in the Paid category while giving you a higher volume of sales. This volume of sales will allow your Kindle eBook to reclaim its spot (or land on a better spot) on the Top 100 bestsellers lists for its categories.

Method #44: Network with other people at events

If you interact with the right people in your community, you may be able to get numerous overnight Kindle eBook sales from your community alone. In order to get these sales, you need to network with other people at events in your community. All you need to do is network at events that revolve around your niche and talk to the people sitting next to you. Soon enough, you will be telling these people about everything you do, and those people will be doing the same. In the end, you will both exchange contact information and may even get a sale.

How To Make People At The Events More Likely To Download Your Kindle eBook

When you tell people about your Kindle eBook, they need to have a reason to buy it right when they get home from the event. Telling everyone that your Kindle eBook is there will not be enough to get the sale. You need to know the right techniques in order to get more sales.

The first technique is to come out as a nice person (which you should be in the first place). If the person you are talking to does not see you as a nice person, then all of the other techniques will be ineffective. People are more likely to buy from nice people. Just be polite and know your social etiquette so the people you talk to will like you.

The second technique is to either have a free promotion or discount for your Kindle eBook live while you are at the event. Having a free promotion or discount for your Kindle eBook will make buying your Kindle eBook become more urgent. Instead of waiting a few days to buy your Kindle eBook (and then forget about it all together), people have a stronger desire to buy your Kindle eBook because of the urgency of the discount.

The third and final technique to getting more sales is to not come with a business card. Instead, come with a flyer. Business cards can get misplaced, slip out of a pocket, and be forgotten. However, it is much harder to forget about a flyer primarily because of its size. You also have more space on a flyer to add pictures of social media icons, your Kindle eBooks, and your logo.

Summarizing Methods 36-44

These methods are primarily a way for you to get more reviews. The prelaunch and launch stages are designed to get a big quantity of sales so some of those customers will review your Kindle eBook. After the launch stage takes place, it is important to not forget about your Kindle eBook. After the launch sales die off, your Kindle eBook will slowly drop down in its ranking as new titles take its place. You need to continue using the tools and features mentioned in Methods 26-35 so your Kindle eBooks do not slip too far behind. Contacting customers who left good reviews for your Kindle eBooks will entice those customers to buy Kindle eBooks that you publish in the future, and those customers will also be very likely to leave good reviews for those Kindle eBooks.

Methods 45-53: Getting A Higher Volume Of Sales

For Kindle eBooks, getting a higher volume of sales is better than getting a few sales with big commissions. It is better for the self-published author when 100 people buy a $2.99 Kindle eBook than when 30 people buy a $9.97 Kindle eBook. A higher volume of sales will possibly lead to more reviews because the entry (price) is more welcoming. While lowering your Kindle eBooks' prices is an obvious starting point, there are other ways to get a higher volume of sales that are not as commonly implemented in the Kindle marketplace.

Method #45: Lower Your Kindle eBooks' Prices

Your Kindle eBook's price has a big impact on how many sales it gets. If you price your Kindle eBook too high, then less people are going to buy it. However, if you price your Kindle eBook too low, people will not be as likely to buy your Kindle eBook. Customers who see a Kindle eBook being sold for $0.99 are quick to question the quality of that Kindle eBook.

The ideal price for a Kindle eBook is $2.99. That way, you make 70% per sale and still get a high volume of sales. There are many successful self-published authors who sell their Kindle eBooks for $2.99 while some go as high as $3.97. Low prices look very attractive to potential customers because a low price is a small investment. If the $2.99 turns out to be a dud, it was still a small investment. However, your job as the author is to make sure none of your Kindle eBooks turn out to be duds. Someone who buys your Kindle eBook can still refund it within 60 days. In addition, the only way you are going to get returning customers is if people like your Kindle eBooks. While it is important to lower your Kindle eBook's prices, it is also important to not forget about quality content.

What Lowering A Kindle eBook's Price Did For Me

When I published my first Kindle eBook, *Honest Ways To Make Money Online*, I had no idea about any of the rules that made self-published authors successful. I decided to price the 32 page eBook for $9.97 so I would be able to make $6.98 per sale. Then I did the math to find out how many sales it would take for me to make $1,000 every month and eventually $100,000 every year.

At the price I set, none of those two things ever happened. In fact, I did not make a single sale. I was shocked that my Kindle eBook did not make a single sale because as a new author, I thought my Kindle eBook was the one that everyone would be buying, even at $9.97.

I noticed the problem within a few weeks and decided to lower the Kindle eBook's price. A few days after I lowered my Kindle eBook's price to $2.99, a sale came in. Sales continued to come in for my Kindle eBook and have now been coming in at a consistent, steady rate.

Although I was at first reluctant to lower my Kindle eBook's price (at the time, I saw this as cutting myself short), I saw a volume of sales come in. In less than a month, I made enough sales for my Kindle eBook to earn well over $6.98. Although I decreased my commission, I was able to get more customers.

Look At Your Competitors' Prices

If you want an idea of how much you should charge for your Kindle eBooks, look at your competitors' prices. When you look at the competitors' prices, be sure to look at self-published Kindle eBooks' prices instead of traditionally published Kindle eBooks' prices. By looking at these prices, you will have an idea of what you need to charge for your Kindle eBooks. When I saw most of my competitors charging $2.99 for similar Kindle eBooks, I lowered my Kindle eBook's price from $9.97 to $2.99. By lowering my Kindle eBook's price to match the competitors' prices, I was able to boost my sales.

In addition to looking at your competitors' prices, you should also look at the products. If your competitors are selling 45 page Kindle eBooks for $2.99, you would have a distinct advantage if you sold a 75 page Kindle eBook for only $2.99 let alone a 100 page Kindle eBook. Another way to beat the competition is by writing a 45 page Kindle eBook and only selling it for $0.99. While page numbers are important, it is also important to never lose sight of quality content. While many self-published authors are writing 45 page Kindle eBooks and selling them for $2.99, those Kindle eBooks are information-packed and tend to have content that is worth more than $2.99. The low price encourages more people to buy those Kindle eBooks. By identifying the average prices of your competitors' Kindle eBooks and amount of pages, you will be able to write Kindle eBooks that give more value to readers than the average competitor's Kindle eBook. I want to emphasize yet again that selling your Kindle eBooks for low prices will allow you to get a volume of sales. That volume of sales is how most self-published authors are able to make over $100,000 every year from selling their Kindle eBooks.

Method #46: Sell A $0.99 Kindle eBook

While selling Kindle eBooks at lower prices will result in more sales, it is very important to have at least one Kindle eBook in your product range that only costs $0.99. Selling a Kindle eBook for $0.99 is a good entry price that will get a higher volume of sales. If your customers like the $0.99 Kindle eBook, then they will be more likely to buy your Kindle eBooks that are $2.99.

Use The $0.99 Kindle eBook To Promote One Of You $2.99 Kindle eBooks

A great way to get more sales with a $0.99 Kindle eBook is to use it to promote another Kindle eBook in your product range worth $2.99. If you have a $2.99 Kindle eBook on fashion that is 100 pages, you can write a 40 page Kindle eBook about fashion tips for beginners and sell it for $0.99. The less expensive Kindle eBook will be the one that gets people to look at your more expensive Kindle eBook. The more a customer looks at your more expensive Kindle eBook about fashion, the more likely that person is going to buy it.

The Ideal Length For A $0.99 Kindle eBook

A Kindle eBook that you sell for $0.99 should not be as long as the other Kindle eBooks you are selling. All $0.99 Kindle eBooks should be at least 30 pages long. If you are writing 100 page Kindle eBooks and want your $0.99 Kindle eBook to be 80 pages, then go for it. Regardless of how long your $0.99 Kindle eBook is, the $0.99 Kindle eBook needs to have quality content so your customers have a good reason to become returning customers. Don't be repetitive and use big words just to reach 30 pages. Anyone can do that. It's the thoughts, ideas, and messages you are able to convey in those 30 or so pages about your niche that will allow you to stand out and get more returning customers.

Method #47: Have A Platinum Priced Product

When I decided to price *Honest Ways To Make Money Online* at $9.97, it was an obvious swing and miss. Although the price and the Kindle eBook did not mix well, you may write a book that you believe is worth $9.97. You may write a 200+ nonfiction Kindle eBook with the best tips in the Kindle marketplace. That can be your platinum priced product: the one that you sell for $9.97.

Having a platinum priced gives you a powerful advantage against the competition. If most of your Kindle eBooks are being sold for $2.99, and you sell one of your Kindle eBooks for $9.97, those Kindle eBooks being sold for $2.99 are going to look a lot cheaper. In this scenario, the customers who buy your Kindle eBooks that are being sold for $2.99 won't think that they are spending $2.99. Instead, the customers will think in the sense that they are saving $6.98 (which conveniently happens to be the commission you would get for a $9.97 Kindle book).

The platinum priced product makes your other products look super inexpensive. Brendon Burchard is a bestselling author, and his Kindle books are over $10. However, Burchard also has a $1,997 training course. All of a sudden, those Kindle eBooks that are worth a little over $10 no longer look expensive. Although people spend a little over $10 to buy his Kindle eBooks, they see it as saving almost $2,000 by not buying the training course. Although Burchard's Kindle eBooks are different from the training course, he is still able to make numerous sales through this method.

Beat Your Competition With A Platinum Product For A Platinum Price
If most of your $2.99 Kindle eBooks are 50-100 pages, write a 250 page Kindle eBook and sell it for $7.77 (no one knows why, but having 7's on the price tag increases conversion). While your customers will know that the 250 page Kindle eBook is jam packed with quality content (hopefully), many of them would prefer to spend their money on less expensive Kindle eBooks. The main reason why self-published authors are able to beat traditionally published authors is because self-published authors can lower their prices. However, many self-published authors make the mistake of not including a platinum priced Kindle eBook on their author page. While

Brendon Burchard implements this tactic with training courses and books, you can implement this tactic solely with Kindle eBooks. Many self-published authors are making the mistake of pricing all of their Kindle eBooks at $2.99 or lower. The problem is that after seeing $2.99 too many times, $2.99 suddenly looks a little more expensive than normal.

Method #48: Over Deliver

No matter what kind of product you are selling, over delivering will allow you to get more sales. If you provide more than your competitor at the same price, more customers are going to buy your Kindle eBook than the competitor's book. By over delivering in your books, your customers will feel really good about their purchase. This good feeling will make some of your customers feel obligated to leave a good review for your Kindle eBook.

Big Promise, Over Deliver

While over delivering is a critical part towards getting more book sales, it is important to remember that it costs money for someone to buy one of your Kindle eBooks. Over deliver is the last half of the slogan, "Under Promise, Over Deliver." As a result, there are too many people who think that under promising and then over delivering is the right approach.
Wrong!
Here is a classic example of where under promising can go horribly wrong. If your friend is at a local restaurant, and you tell your friend that you will arrive two hours from now, chances are your friend will leave the restaurant and ask if you would like to do it again some other time. Even if you were only 5 minutes away from the restaurant and wanted to surprise your friend, you already lost that friend's interest. Now imagine doing that to a customer who does not know you very well. That customer wouldn't

ask if you would like to hang out some other time. That customer would leave, spread the word about you (in a bad way), and never buy another one of your products.

Instead of under promising, why not give the reader a big promise right from the start. Instead of telling your friend that it will take 2 hours for you to get to the restaurant, tell that person it will take you 5 minutes to get to the restaurant. That is already a very strong promise, and your friend will like that a lot. Then, if you show up 2 minutes early, your friend will love you for it.

That's the same thing that you need to do with your customers. You need to give them a big promise in your Kindle eBook's description, and then over deliver by providing more content than you promised.

Method #49: Provide Free Services And Products After You Make The Sale

It seems as if the box of cereal with the prize inside tastes better than the cereal without the prize inside. The idea of giving someone an unexpected prize resulted in more returning customers. Buying another cereal box would result in another free prize. As people started to expect prizes, the value of the prize inside the cereal box slowly diminished.

However, no one is expecting a free prize inside a Kindle eBook. What if you could provide a bonus product or service to your customer for free that they were not expecting after they bought the Kindle eBook?

The better your free prize is, the more valuable it will be. What if you gave away a training course with four videos instead of a training course with three videos? What if you gave away two related PDFs instead of just one? The possibilities are endless, and the thought of getting a free prize will encourage a customer to come back for more.

Make The Free Prizes In Your Books Different

The reason the cereal boxes with the free prize were so popular was because you could get a different prize each time. If there were six free prizes, people who bought the cereal boxes would want to collect all of the free prizes. If each of your Kindle eBooks contain a different free prize, some of your customers would buy your Kindle eBooks just to collect all of the free prizes.

What Free Prizes Should You Offer?

The only problem with offering a free prize in a Kindle eBook is that you neither want to give too much nor too little away. Giving away too much free content will discourage people from buying your paid content. If your free prize is too valuable, your customers will be happy with it and not buy any of your other Kindle eBooks. However, it is important to remember that your free prize still needs to be good enough for your customer to want another one. If the cereal boxes had broken toys, those brands would have gotten less returning customers. Since you are creating different free prizes for each of your Kindle eBooks, creating free prizes that do not take a lot of time to make will allow you to save time and still provide enough value for your customers.

Offer Free Prizes That Promote Your Other Kindle eBooks

Another great way to boost your sales is by offering a free prize that promotes your other books. For some of the people who already buy one of your Kindle eBooks, mentioning your other Kindle eBook may be all it takes to get another sale. By writing a diverse range of Kindle eBooks that are all focused on the same niche, you will be able to mention books that people will want to read.

Method #50: Give Your Customers A Free Training Course

I'm sure there are people wondering if they can give away a free Kindle eBook or a single video instead of an entire training course. Giving away a free training course is another way for you to over deliver to the customer. A free training course allows the customer to get more than what they bargained for. All you need to do for a free training course is to create a training series with 5-10 videos that are 5-10 minutes each. The more you offer in your free training course, the more likely your customer will become a returning customer.

The advantage of offering a free training course is that you still make a profit. While giving someone a physical book costs money (shipping, handling, and all of that fun stuff), giving someone an online training course does not cost you anything. Since people have to buy your Kindle eBook to get access to the training course, you will still make money. Some people will buy your Kindle eBook just to get your training course for free.

Case Study: How Jeremy Schoemaker Effectively Used This Method
The inspiration for this method came from Jeremy Schoemaker. His book, *Nothing's Changed But My Change*, went on Amazon's bestsellers list. In order to keep his book on the bestsellers list longer and get more sales at the same time, Schoemaker decided that every new customer would also get free access to his $197 training course. In addition, any past customers could also get the entire training course for free. This training course has over 50 videos with numerous hours of content. Not only was Schoemaker offering his customers free access to a training course, but he was also offering his customers free access to a top-level training course. His book stayed on the bestsellers list for weeks and now has over 50 reviews.

But that's not all. Some of the people who bought Jeremy's training course left reviews for the training course and bought his other training courses as well. Imagine what would happen if you offered this kind of deal after publishing 10 Kindle eBooks and creating 3 training courses. You would get a swarm of returning customers. Offering the free training course will also get you closer to the three sales rule.

Method #51: Create Bundles

Another great method to sell more Kindle eBooks is by creating bundles. Bundles allow you to put some of your Kindle eBooks together to create one giant Kindle eBook. While you sell the individual Kindle eBooks, you can offer the bundle at an enticing price. If three Kindle eBooks are in the bundle, and those Kindle eBooks are $2.99 each, you can sell the bundle for $5.99. That way, you make a bigger commission for every sale, and the price tells the customer that with this bundle, they are buying two of your Kindle eBooks and getting a third one for free.

When you create bundles, you need to make sure that the three Kindle eBooks you put in the bundle are very similar. A three Kindle eBook bundle with 1 Kindle eBook about social media marketing, a second Kindle eBook about plagiarism, and a third Kindle eBook about a fictional story will not work. If you write about social media marketing, your bundle should consist of 1 Kindle eBook about Twitter marketing, another Kindle eBook about Pinterest marketing, and a third Kindle eBook about Facebook marketing. Since these three Kindle eBooks are similar, and your customers get them at a lower price than if they bought all three individual Kindle eBooks, they will be more likely to buy the entire bundle than buying each individual Kindle eBook.

The Bundle Also Promotes Your Individual Kindle eBooks

There will be some people who look at your bundle and only want one of the three Kindle eBooks. Only buying one of the Kindle eBooks allows the customer to save money and gives you an extra sale. People who would have skipped over your individual Kindle eBook now have a strong need to buy it. The $2.99 Kindle eBook suddenly appears as a discount compared to the bundle. The more discounts you give your customers, the more likely you are going to make the sale.

The Bundle Acts As Your Platinum Priced Product

Since you are charging more for the bundle than your other Kindle eBooks, the bundle will act as your platinum priced product. While making $2.99 look a lot cheaper, the bundle is also the ideal option for anyone who wants to buy all three of your Kindle eBooks. Having a bundle will allow the customer to feel like he is getting the best deal no matter which of your Kindle eBook(s) he purchases.

Method #52: Diversify Your Product Range

In Method #15, I discussed why focusing on one niche is powerful. Although focusing on one niche is important, it is also important to diversify your product range. Let's say your niche is developing a strong presence on the web. There are a lot of topics to choose from that allow you to develop a stronger presence on the web. You can write Kindle eBooks about social media, blogging, and boosting sales. When you write Kindle eBooks about social media, one of them can be about Twitter while another one can be about Pinterest. It is possible to diversify your product while still focusing on one niche.

Diversifying Your Product Range Allows You To Be More Specific

While blogging is a big niche, some people want to learn about improving their SEO while other people want to learn what goes into writing a quality blog post. Writing Kindle eBooks on those different topics will allow you to attract more customers. Being specific with your Kindle eBooks allows you to fulfill specific needs. Fulfilling specific needs is what will allow your Kindle eBooks to make more sales. Instead of asking yourself what topic you should write about, ask yourself how you can narrow down the topic to focus on specific needs. I could have wrote this entire Kindle eBook about being successful on the Kindle and gone into detail about formatting, how to publish your content with KDP, and all of that fun stuff. Instead, I only wrote about the different methods self-published authors can use to get more sales. It is always possible to turn one Kindle eBook idea into multiple Kindle eBooks.

Method #53: Turn Your Readers Into Returning Customers

They say that 80% of your revenue comes from 20% of your customers. Although that probably won't be the case for your Kindle eBooks, the popular saying emphasizes how important it is to turn your readers into returning customers. Imagine what would happen if 100 customers bought 5 of your Kindle eBooks. That would be 500 sales, and if you make an average of $2.02 per sale, that's an extra $1,010! Imagine what would happen if you increased those numbers. As you continue to write Kindle eBooks and get more sales, it will be your returning customers that allow your Kindle eBooks to have excellent prelaunches and leave good reviews.

Going More In Depth About The Three Sales Rule

I have mentioned the three sales rule a few times in this Kindle eBook. In order for the three sales rule to work effectively, you need to have a lot of Kindle eBooks. If you turn someone into a customer for life, it is better to have 10 Kindle eBooks available than it is to have 5 Kindle eBooks available. That's a difference of 5 sales for each customer for life, and as you get more customers for life, those numbers go up.

The great part is that the KDP Free Promotion and the Kindle Countdown Deals count towards the three sales rule. If you want to get the three sales rule done in 1 day, you need to have 2 of your Kindle eBooks under the KDP Free Promotion and 1 of your Kindle eBooks under the Kindle Countdown Deal. Another option you have is putting 1 Kindle eBook under the KDP Free Promotion and 2 of your Kindle eBooks under the Kindle Countdown Deal. You will need to have additional Kindle eBooks available for sale if you plan to turn someone from a potential customer to a customer for life in 1 day.

Get Readers To Subscribe To Your Blog

Steve Scott is a successful self-published author who introduces a free product at the start of all of his Kindle eBooks. He puts this product on the first page of his Kindle eBooks because anyone who looks inside one of his Kindle eBooks with the free preview also gets access to the free product. All you need to do to gain access to the free product is by subscribing to Steve's blog.

This smart tactic is one of the reasons why Steve makes 6 figures every year. By growing a big list and giving away a free product, people on the list decided they wanted to buy one of Steve's Kindle eBooks. Then, some of those people became customers for life and left positive reviews for Steve's Kindle eBooks.

In order to build an audience who may be eager buy your Kindle eBooks the moment they come out, you need to get more subscribers for your blog. As you get more subscribers, more people pay attention to the content on your blog. When you write the blog post about your new Kindle eBooks, then your subscribers and people who visit your blog will buy those new Kindle eBooks. In addition, some of these people will buy your older Kindle eBooks as well.

Write A Kindle eBook Series

A great way to get returning customers is by writing a Kindle eBook series. If readers enjoyed the first Kindle eBook in the series, chances are the reader will buy the second Kindle eBook in your series as well. By writing Kindle eBook series, you will make the three sales rule easier to reach. In addition, as your series continues to grow, more people will buy your Kindle eBooks to catch up. No matter how *Star Wars VII* turns out, millions of people will watch it. Since many people bought all six Star Wars movies or have seen all of them, *Star Wars VII* will be a very popular movie.

One of the best examples of a successful book series is *Harry Potter*. Because of this seven book series, J.K. Rowling was able to go from being homeless to living life as a billionaire. Throughout the course of the series, over 400 million *Harry Potter* books were purchased. Although that indicates the books were very popular, the big number also has a lot to do with returning customers. If a customer bought three of J.K. Rowling's *Harry Potter* books, that customer would buy the other four books as well. Now let's use big numbers. Assuming that 20 million people bought three books in the series and then bought the other four, that adds up to 140 million sales. Although this is on quite a big scale, it does show how easy it is for a book series to get returning customers and get you more sales.

Summarizing Methods 45-53

Making money for each sale is important, but getting a volume of sales will allow you to connect with more people and get more reviews. You should focus on keeping most of your Kindle eBooks at $2.99 (at least 80% of them), have some of those Kindle eBooks get sold for $0.99, and create a bundle containing three of your Kindle eBooks for just $5.99. Customers will see your bundle as a sweet deal, and if they don't want the bundle, your $0.99 and $2.99 Kindle eBooks will look more affordable.

Methods 54-60: Become The Celebrity Of Your Niche

The most successful self-published authors are the celebrities of their niche. They don't have followings like all of the music and reality TV stars, but they have a big audience of the people that matter to them--targeted people. Becoming the celebrity of your niche will automatically make you stand out and allow you to get hundreds of sales on the day one of your Kindle eBooks gets published. Reaching celebrity status in your niche also has other perks such as more opportunities, more revenue, and more financial flexibility.

Method #54: Boost Your Credibility

Customers don't just buy anyone's Kindle eBook. They buy Kindle eBooks written by the authors who have the most credibility. Customers are more likely to buy the YouTube Kindle eBook with 20 positive reviews than they are to buy the YouTube Kindle eBook about the same topic with 1 positive review.

Credibility is one of the most important parts of making the sale because credibility increase trustworthiness. If you were creating a championship team for the NBA, and you could either have LeBron James or a high school student play on your team, you would take LeBron James. LeBron has more credibility since he plays at a more professional level. You trust LeBron James to make the three point shots more than you trust the high school student.

The same applies to Kindle eBook sales. People are more likely to trust the person with 500,000 Twitter followers than they are to trust the person with 10,000 Twitter followers. Since the person with 500,000 Twitter followers is theoretically on the bigger stage, customers tend to expect more from that person. Customers also tend to expect more from the author who has written 10 bestselling Kindle eBooks than the author who has only written 1 bestselling Kindle eBook.

How To Boost Your Credibility

There are a plethora of ways to boost your credibility. Here are some of the numerous ways to boost your credibility.

1. Grow your following on your social networks.
2. Build your niche into a full-time income, and let people know about it.
3. Get over 100,000 blog visitors every year.
4. Get interviewed by multiple people.
5. Do public speaking.
6. Get good reviews.
7. Increase your Klout Score.
8. Have more than 10 Kindle eBooks.
9. Get featured on *Forbes*, *The Associated Press*, or another big media outlet.

There are other ways to boost your credibility, but these are the big ones. There is no limit to how much credibility anyone can have. The more credibility you have, the more sales you are going to make.

Method #55: Answer Questions On Yahoo! Answers

Yahoo! Answers gets over 50 millions visitors every day. That's a lot of people, but that's also a lot of people who have questions related to your niche. When people ask questions, they are looking for experts to answer their questions. That's where you come in. If someone does not know how something works in your niche, show that person the way. When you answer the question, be sure to include a URL to your blog. When the person clicks on the link to your blog, that person will be very likely to subscribe to your blog. As the connection develops, that person who asked the question that you answered may decide to buy one of your Kindle eBooks a few weeks or months later.

Answering questions on Yahoo! Answers also has some long-term effects. The question that one person asks is the question that hundreds of thousands of people had but did not ask. Since Yahoo! Answers gets over 50 million visitors every day, some of those visitors will be looking at the answer you submitted. When they look at the answer you submitted, they will also be likely to subscribe to your blog for free content and eventually buy your Kindle eBooks. In addition, providing a link to your blog will count towards a backlink and boost your blog's SEO. Answering questions on Yahoo! Answers also boosts your credibility.

How Many Questions Should You Answer Every Day

The more questions you answer on Yahoo! Answers, the more connections you are going to make. However, crafting a good answer takes time, and it also takes some time to find people who are asking the right questions that you can answer. It is important to remember that the right questions are the ones that revolve around your niche. Only answer social media questions if you are a social media expert, and only answer fashion questions if your are in the fashion business. When someone looks at your blog, you won't be able to grab their attention.

You should answer 10 questions that revolve around your niche every week. That means for the most part you will be answering one question every day while answering two questions on some days. You may also decide to answer all 10 questions in 1 day. The schedule you use to implement this method is entirely up to you as long as you are answering 10 questions every week. Answering that many questions will allow you to make more connections and be a well-known person in the Yahoo! Answers community (but more importantly, you will become a well-known expert in your niche).

Method #56: Get Interviewed

Getting interviewed will have a long-term impact on your sales. When someone interviews you, you get a different kind of exposure. Sure, the interview will bring more traffic to your blog and get you a few followers on your social networks. However, this kind of exposure will show people that you are an expert in your niche.

Not everyone in your niche gets interviewed. The people who are getting interviewed are the ones on top of their game. The self-published authors who are getting interviewed about their success are the ones who are making $100,000 every year. The sports athletes who get interviewed the most are the ones playing at the professional level.

As you get interviewed more often, big media outlets will start to pay attention. After appearing in enough places, you may get a call from *Forbes* asking for an interview. When I first started my journey, no one was interviewing me. I was just another small fish in a ginormous pond. As I started to build my presence and get more exposure, more interview requests came in.

How To Boost Your Chances Of Getting Interviewed

The media will not interview someone just for the sake of giving that person more exposure. Names don't just get pulled out of a hat. The entire process is a two way street. Even big media outlets like *The New York Times* want more readers. Big media outlets only interview the people who they believe will have a big impact on their readership. That means you need to have a remarkable story in order to get interviewed by anyone, let alone the big media outlets.

As you become more successful and further build your presence on the web, people will start to notice. That's how you get your first couple of interviews. However, in order to make the main stream, you need to be better than the people in your niche at something who also got their first couple of interviews. Whether you write content more frequently, get better results, or have a more remarkable (but true) story, then you will be more likely to get interviewed. Basically, you want to stand out if you want to be interviewed many times. As you get interviewed more often, big media outlets will eventually notice you.

How To Get Big Media Outlets To Know About You Faster

If you want big media outlets to notice you faster, you need to directly contact them. At either the top or bottom of a big media outlet's website, there will be a way for you to contact them. Submitting your story to these big media outlets allows them to notice you faster.

However, you do not want to send your story to a big media outlet too early. Just because you sent your story over to a big media outlet does not mean that big media outlet will use your story. The big media outlets get flooded with emails, and if your story isn't as remarkable as their standard, that big media outlet won't publish your story. Start by building your presence and then send your story to big media outlets. The more remarkable your story is, the more likely a big media outlet is to write about you. Instead of pitching your story to big media outlets right now, wait a few months for your presence to grow larger and then pitch your story to big media outlets.

How To Get Featured On Big Media Outlets Without A Remarkable Story

In order to get an entire article written about you on a big media outlet, you need to have a remarkable story. However, not everyone has a story remarkable enough to take up an entire article. Luckily, there is a way to get featured on a big media outlet without a remarkable story. All you need is expertise and certain qualifications.

If you want to get featured in an article from a big media outlet, you need to use HARO. HARO (Help A Reporter Out) shows you a list of big media outlets who are looking for people like you to send pitches for an article. If the journalist likes your pitch, that journalist will talk about you for a small portion of the article. Getting that extra exposure is still very powerful. That's how I got in the *U.S. News World Report* money section. One of their journalists was writing an article about three simple ways to get better time management. One of my tips happened to fit the bill, and I was one of the people who got featured in that article.

While you are doing the work to enhance your results and make your story more remarkable, this is an easy way to get big media outlets to promote you. When big media outlets promote you in an article, you will be able to tell your visitors and followers that you were featured on a big media outlet. Being featured on a big media outlet makes your story more remarkable because it shows that one of the big names decided to pay attention to what you are doing. Getting featured on big media outlets works like a chain effect. Once you get featured on one big media outlet, more people will come to you asking if they can interview you.

Method #57: Interview Other People

While getting interviewed is a great way to get more Kindle eBook sales, interviewing other people will also boost your Kindle eBook sales and exposure. Just like being interviewed, the process of interviewing other people will also have a long-term effect on your sales. You may not see growth right away, but you will start to see a very noticeable growth in sales a few months later.

When you interview someone, that person is very likely to share the interview on their social networks. While the person you interviewed shows off the interview they had, your blog also gets more traffic. In addition, some of the people who like the person you interviewed will subscribe to your blog. Some of those people are also likely to share that blog post. The reason you get more traffic is because the people who like the person you interviewed now head over to your blog to see the interview. These people want to know what questions you asked and see how the interviewee responded.

Choose The Right People To Interview

In order to get the most exposure from the interview, choose to interview people who have a strong influence. The more followers and traffic that person gets, the more exposure you will get if the interview goes through. While visibility is important, you also want to choose someone who has a remarkable story. If this person's remarkable story grabs your attention, chances are it also grabs the attention of the people who are subscribed to his blog.

In addition, the people who you interview must be in your niche. If you interview someone outside of your niche, then you will lose people's attention. By interviewing someone in your niche, you will also be able to ask better questions which brings forth better answers. A interview that was well conducted will get attention.

Imagine What Would Happen If You Interviewed 100 People With Over 10,000 Followers Each

That would be a lot of interviews, but your part is easy. All you have to do is ask if the person would like to be interviewed and then send them some questions. If you duplicated that 100 times to people who had 10,000 followers each, you would be able to get thousands of extra visitors. Some of the interviewees will share the interview more than once on their social networks. Put together, those 10,000 followers from 100 accounts add up to 1 million people. That's an extra million people who get to see your message. Although few of those people would click on any of the links, you can definitely expect to get well over 1,000 visitors just from those interviews. If you continue to conduct interviews with influential people in your niche, it is easy to imagine going viral. Now that you can imagine what would happen if you interviewed 100 people with over 10,000 followers each, imagine what would happen if those 100 interviewees had 100,000 followers each. There's a lot of potential to get more exposure, and this exposure will lead to more people buying your Kindle eBooks. Some people will buy your Kindle eBooks just because that person liked the way you conducted the interview.

Method #58: Strive To Be Different With Creative Marketing

One of the best ways to get more Kindle eBook sales is to have creative marketing. This kind of marketing is different from the typical choices of marketing. While some people market their Kindle eBooks by sending emails to various blogs and bookstores, others are doing the same things but with a twist. For Seth Godin, that twist was selling his book, *Purple Cow*, in a purple milk carton. He also sold his book *Free Prize Inside* in a cereal box with a Seth Godin action figure. Those are two marketing strategies that are creative, different, and remarkable in the process.

There Is No Answer Except For The One You Come Up With

Creative marketing is not something with steps, how-to's, and bullet points. Creative marketing requires that you come up with a brilliant idea and use it to market your Kindle eBooks. The easiest way to come up with a creative marketing strategy is by looking at past strategies. Examine the ones that you liked the most and then combine elements of those strategies together into your strategy. Then, weigh the pros and cons of your strategy and implement the strategy that you are the most confident about.

Don't Go Out Of Hand With Creative Marketing

Creative marketing is doing something different. However, it is easy to be different. It is easy to do the trailer of your Kindle eBook with a sock in your mouth. That's different, but it's not a difference that people are going to like. Do not be different just for the sake of being different. Coming up with a creative marketing strategy that makes no sense so you can say you do creative marketing for your Kindle eBook will not get you far. If you cannot think of a way to use creative marketing to promote your Kindle eBook, then that's okay. However, as you write more Kindle eBooks, learn more about your niche, and continue to look at past examples, you will eventually come up with your own version of creative marketing and sell your Kindle eBook in an unprecedented way.

Method #59: Be An Effective Storyteller

It's hard to imagine anyone going far without a good story. Brendon Burchard has a story of going from having debt to the 7 figure club. Jeremy Schoemaker has the story of weighing 420 pounds and living on a friend's couch. Now his blog generates millions of dollars every year. Chances are you also have a story. Even if you don't think you have a story, you have one. Many people cut themselves short and think that what they do is not extraordinary.

How To Think Of A Good (But True) Story

Although some people will already know what their story is, other people do not know the story they will tell right now. The entire story you will tell needs to include how you started and be combined with a remarkable story. Having kids while pursuing $100K every year is a remarkable story. Getting fired from multiple jobs and then choosing yourself instead of giving other people the choice of having you is another remarkable story. When you tell this remarkable story, you need to make sure it is true. Don't tell anyone that you lived on a friend's couch if that never happened.

Method #60: Wow Your Readers With Your Credentials

We all have our own set of credentials. In order to make your credentials rise above your competitors' credentials, your credentials need to wow your readers. The credentials that "wow readers" are the ones that few people have accomplished. No one is saying, "Wow, that person is an author." They may say things like, "Wow, that person who used to be broke is now a multimillionaire living in a mansion." The more you separate yourself from others, the stronger your credentials will be.

How To Give Yourself More Credentials That Wow People

Giving yourself credentials forces you to live up to your those credentials. You also need to have credentials that people would pay attention to, and there is an easy set of rules to implement in order to get those "wow" credentials. All you need to do is look at the people in your niche. Chances are most or all of the 1.8% of self-published authors making six figures every year have similar credentials. These self-published authors may have won several awards, write 1 blog post every day, and wrote bestselling Kindle eBooks just to name a few credentials.

What you need to do is look at all of those credentials and identify what credentials that are worth being credible for are missing. In addition, you can do one thing better than your competitors. Maybe you feel the need to publish 1 Kindle eBook every week instead of every month. Maybe you feel the need to launch 1 training course every month. Doing those things boosts your credibility because only a few people do those things. Since few people do the same things that you do, those are the credentials that wow people.

Where To Show People Your Credentials

The best places to show people your credentials are on your blog, social networks, and Amazon author page. People will not be interested in reading about your credentials in your Kindle eBook's free preview. People want to get an idea of the contents your Kindle eBook contains, not your life story. If people buy your Kindle eBook and decide they want to be returning customers, these people will go to your Amazon author page to see your Kindle eBooks. By seeing your Kindle eBooks, these people will also see and most likely read your bio. Showing your credentials at these strategic locations will encourage more people to buy your Kindle eBooks the first time and eventually become returning customers.

Summarizing Methods 54-60

Boosting your credibility is the most important way to become the celebrity of your niche. It's cool when someone has over 10,000 Facebook likes but a lot cooler when someone has over 100,000 Facebook likes. While big (but not fake) numbers play a part in credibility, your expertise also plays a role in your credibility. Getting interviewed and interviewing other people tells other people that you are good enough to do both of those things. In addition, when you answer someone's question on Yahoo! Answers (or Wiki Answers) in great detail with the right information, the people who view that question will see your response. Those people will see you as a person in your niche with a lot of knowledge, and as a result, your credibility goes up. The more your credibility goes up, the closer you get to stardom in your niche.

Methods 61-66: Learn More About Your Niche & Get Inspired

Becoming a successful self-published author is not a sprint. It is a very long marathon. Like all marathons, this one has a finish line in which you will be making $100,000 every year by crossing that finish line. The best part about this type of marathon is that once you cross this finish line, you can constantly raise the bar higher and increase your revenue.

In order to get to the finish line, you need to learn more about your niche and get inspired. In a real marathon, runners get inspired by the thousands of cheering people on the sidelines. For a self-published author, reading about a successful self-published author's story is very inspirational and can also teach you new lessons about your niche.

Method #61: Read Other People's Success Stories

In one of Tony Robbins' motivational videos, he discussed the four elements of success. One of those elements was the need to see potential. Five years after Roger Bannister became the first person to run the mile in under four minutes, 20 athletes broke the four minute barrier for the mile. When Roger Bannister broke the four minute mile barrier, the 20 athletes saw the potential. Before Roger Bannister, everyone thought it was impossible to run a mile in under four minutes.

New self-published authors often get faced with this issue. Constantly getting told, "There's potential in self-publishing," is not convincing enough. Instead, you need to look at the success stories of self-published authors. Earlier in this Kindle eBook, I mentioned Steve Scott who promotes his Kindle eBooks to a giant email list. In less than two years, Steve Scott went from having no Kindle eBooks to becoming a part of the 6 figure club because of his Kindle eBooks. Steve Scott now makes over $250,000 from his Kindle eBooks every year. Imagine what you would be able to do with earnings like that. That's the entire point of a success story. Someone else's success story makes you wonder what you would do if you were the one making that much money. When you see the potential and start to crave success, that will encourage you to put more work into your writing. It is these components that creates the winning mindset for a self-published author.

Is There Such Thing As Reading Too Many Success Stories

Reading success stories will invigorate you and fill you with a new craving for success. However, there are some people who will read 10 (or more) success stories and start living in the fantasy. While it is important to envision yourself becoming successful, some people live in the fantasy too early. The people who live in the fantasy think about what will happen when they make the 6 figure club instead of doing the work that will allow them to reach the 6 figure club. Self-publishing can be brutal. In a humongous pond, the big fish are the role models. While we can admire them for as long as we want, writing Kindle eBooks and getting more sales is the only way you are going to be a big fish in the Amazon pond (also known as a giant ocean).

Success Stories Contain Valuable Tips

Almost every success story I have read contains tips from that self-published author. One of the most common questions big fish in the Amazon pond get is related to getting more sales. That's why many self-published authors leave a method at the end of their interview to boost sales. In addition, the person interviewing the successful self-published author tends to ask how self-published authors can get more sales.

Method #62: Look At Your Competitors And See What You Are Missing

When I am thinking about good ideas for my Kindle eBooks, I look at the competition and see what kinds of Kindle eBooks are in demand. Looking at competitors' Kindle eBooks gives me an idea of which of my Kindle eBook ideas can become very successful. While searching around, I noticed that many competitors wrote Kindle eBooks that taught people how they can self-publish more Kindle eBooks faster or write more words in a given day. I eventually wrote a Kindle eBook on the same concept but with different methods. I also noticed a Kindle eBook about getting more Kindle sales, and I responded by writing this Kindle eBook which has more methods than any other Kindle eBook that I have stumbled across on Amazon.

There are Kindle eBook topics out there that you competitors have already written that you can write on your own without needing to read that competitor's Kindle eBook. I'm sure there are plenty of people who can write a Kindle eBook on Facebook without reading a competitor's Kindle eBook first. Browsing through Amazon to find your competitors' Kindle eBooks is just a way for you to gather ideas and see which ones work.

How To Find Your Competitors' Kindle eBooks

Finding your competitors' Kindle eBooks is a very easy process. All you need to do is use Amazon's Kindle eBook search engine and enter your niche as the search term. Then, all of your competitors' Kindle eBooks will come up. When your competitors' Kindle eBooks come up, the most popular ones will appear on the first page. You can use these Kindle eBooks as inspiration for your next Kindle eBook.

Look At The Descriptions

Chances are you probably wrote a Kindle eBook and want to get an edge on the competition. Instead of trying to get an edge on the competition, it is important to realize that the most popular Kindle eBooks in your niche already have an edge on you. These Kindle eBooks have more reviews and get more daily sales than your Kindle eBook. In order to make your Kindle eBook successful, you need to look at the description for your competitors' Kindle eBooks. No matter how closely related your Kindle eBook is, copying and pasting is never the solution, and it will end up hurting you in the long run. However, if you look at patterns in the descriptions and create a description that combines elements of your competitors' descriptions, you will be able to create a description that generates more sales.

Look At Anything Else That Is Important

Anything that the competitor is doing that you like but are not doing is something important. Some competitors have self-published 20 Kindle eBooks, and by self-publishing 20 of your own quality Kindle eBooks, you will be able to catch up to those competitors. Maybe your competitor has an inspirational video on their Author Page that gives the customer a good feeling--the good feeling that makes the customer click the Buy Now button. Ignoring the competition is an impossibility, and it is better to learn from the competition than it is to be envious of the competitors who are on Page 1 for their keywords.

Method #63: Learn From The Statistics You Currently Have

There are many people who are rushing to find different ways to get more Kindle eBook sales without looking at their statistics. Your sales report on

KDP may hold the secrets to your success. Your statistics will allow you to identify when you got the most amount of sales. The reason I know the KDP Free Promotion works is because after running it the first time, I got daily sales.

The lesson I learned from this part of my statistics is that the KDP Free Promotion leads to more sales in the long-term. Since then, I have been running Free Promotions for some of my other Kindle eBooks. When the promotion expires, I get more paid unit sales than I was getting before the free promotion started.

In addition, your statistics will show you which countries you are getting the most sales from. Many people in the United States think that Amazon.com is the international domain name. However, there are different Amazon sites for the United Kingdom, India, Japan, France, and other places in the world. Although customers can buy the same products, currency and your Kindle eBook's sales rank will vary in the countries that use Amazon (almost all of them). When I started to get daily sales, I learned from my statistics that most of those sales came from customers in the United Kingdom. Seeing this statistic gave me more confidence in my self-publishing career. While I saw the U.S. rank go up, the rank for my Kindle eBook in the United Kingdom was going down, and my Kindle eBook eventually made it to the Top 100 List for one of its categories.

The statistics will also allow you to see which of your Kindle eBooks is making the most sales. If your Kindle eBook about Facebook is making the most sales, your audience is filled with people who want to learn more about Facebook. By identifying what a bulk of your customers like, you will identify your next Kindle eBook. By writing another Kindle eBook about Facebook, you will get more returning customers. As they leave good reviews, more people will buy your Kindle eBook. Then, some of those customers will go back to your first Kindle eBook about Facebook and buy that one as well. In this case, the statistics allow you to identify the Kindle eBooks you need to write about in order to get more sales.

Method #64: Ask Yourself If You Would Buy Your Own Kindle eBook If You Were Not The Author

One simple question, if answered honestly, has the power to identify how confident you truly feel about your Kindle eBook. If you would buy your own Kindle eBook if you were the customer, then your Kindle eBook is one step closer to getting a lot of sales. If you would not buy your own Kindle eBook, then there is something wrong. If your Kindle eBook is already published and you have come to the conclusion that you would not buy it, then you need to do a revision so you can put a Kindle eBook up for sale that you would be proud of. Confidence plays a big part in your ability to write more Kindle eBooks faster and sell the ones that you have. Asking yourself this question throughout the writing process will make you write better content. Many people only think about the money when they write their Kindle eBooks. However, if you constantly ask yourself this question, the money gets pushed to the side. Asking yourself this question will allow you to write the kind of content that you would want to buy, and as a result, it would also result in the kind of content that potential customers would love to buy.

Method #65: Identify The Main Reasons Why You Are Currently Not Making More Sales

The results from this activity depend on the way you treat it. Many people are quick to only say that they don't have enough traffic. However, I ask you to dig deeper. There may be multiple reasons why you are not making more sales and are not yet in the 6 figure club. If you look at what you currently have and go through the methods in this Kindle eBook, you will be able to identify the things that you don't have. I remember when I started my career as a self-published author that these were the main reasons why I was not getting more sales.

1. **I did not have a strong enough presence**. I solved this problem by growing a powerful presence on Twitter. Now I gain over 500 followers every day, and it shows no signs of stopping!

2. **I did not have enough Kindle eBooks available**. I now publish 1 Kindle eBook every month. In addition, the Kindle eBooks I am publishing are now longer than the Kindle eBooks I was publishing before.

Those were the two main reasons why I was currently not making more sales than I made at the time. I could have added small reasons such as not having enough time to write or not being on a bestsellers list. Having too many reasons creates an overwhelming problem that seems impossible to get solved. By only identifying two main reasons instead of 10 minuscule reasons that had a tiny impact (or none at all), I was able to identify what needed the most attention. Out of all of the reasons, my presence on the web and my writing needed the most attention. It is better to have 2-3 reasons for why you are not making more sales than it is to come up with 10 different reasons. Coming up with 10 reasons alone takes too much time, but having to do something about those 10 reasons takes even more time.

What To Do After You Identify The Main Reasons
Identifying the main reasons is not going to get you more sales. Identifying is easy. Doing is hard. You need to come up with a plan to address and solve these issues. If you know why your Kindle eBooks are not getting a lot of sales, then you know *exactly* what you need to do to get more sales. When you create a plan, you need to create a day by day plan with weekly

goals. Here is an example of the plan I created when I realized I was not writing enough Kindle eBooks:

1. Finish writing 1 Kindle eBook every month.
2. These Kindle eBooks must contain at least 20,000 words.
3. I must finish writing the Kindle eBook within 2 weeks so I can proofread it.
4. That means 10,000 words every week. 1,500 words every day gets me to 10,500 words which would put me at 500 words above my goal (that's a good thing).
5. After those two weeks, I need to proofread the entire Kindle eBook in two days.
6. After that, I need to read the entire Kindle eBook out loud and make any necessary corrections for three days.
7. Finally, I publish my Kindle eBook, market it, and then think of my next Kindle eBook during my week off.

This plan allowed me to solve one of my main problems. By creating a similar plan and crunching the numbers to come up with a reasonable rate (something that you can do that brings discomfort but does not overwhelm you), you will be able to solve the problems that are preventing you from getting more sales.

Method #66: Be Persistent

No matter what you do in life, you must have persistence. The only reason there are some self-published authors who are in the 6 figure club is because those self-published authors were persistent. Some of these authors started off by only making $25 every month from their Kindle eBook sales. Some self-published authors made less on their first month. During my first month, I made a whooping $6. Now I make much more than that every month.

Whether you are currently making $8 every month from your Kindle Kindle eBooks or $100 every month, persistence will allow you to go further. Right now, you are following the steps of self-published authors who make 6 figures every year. These are the steps that they take, and you'll be surprised with how many of these steps you have taken as well.

1. **The decision to start**. You either made that decision earlier or made that decision when you bought this Kindle eBook.

2. **Write a Kindle eBook**. You can write your first 15,000 word Kindle eBook in just 1 month at a very comfortable 500 words every day. Soon, you will be able to write 7,000 words every day.

3. **Publish that Kindle eBook**. Writing it is the hard part. Publishing it with KDP is much easier.

4. **Make the first sale**. If your only sales are when friends bought your Kindle eBook, that's great. If a stranger bought your Kindle eBook, then you're in business. Getting the first sale will definitely bring forth a lot of joy.

5. **Continue writing Kindle eBooks**. The moment you publish your second Kindle eBook, you allow people to become returning customers. In addition, if customers know you write 1 Kindle eBook every month, they'll be back for the next Kindle eBook that you write.

6. **Learn more about getting sales**. You have been doing that by reading this Kindle eBook.

7. **Implement those tactics and get more sales**. Implementing is the hardest part, but it separates 6 figure self-published authors from the average.

8. **Keep on implementing those tactics**. By implementing these tactics and staying true to the goal, you will eventually become a part of the 6 figure club.

Everyone forgets that even the self-published authors in the 6 figure club struggled at one point to make a single sale. Chances are you have taken

2-5 of these steps already. You may be more than halfway there. This entire Kindle eBook lays out what you need to know about getting more sales. The research has been done for you. All you need to do now is continue implementing these tactics and write more Kindle eBooks. Whether it takes you a few months or two years, you may end up in the 6 figure club.

Summarizing Methods 61-66

Learning more about your niche and getting inspired over a long period of time will eventually allow you to cross the finish line and make a full-time income from your self-published Kindle eBooks. Persistence has the potential to make you go from making under $100 every month from your Kindle eBooks to thousands of dollars every month. Enjoy the journey and realize that by implementing these methods and staying persistent, your self-publishing career can become a very successful one.

Methods 67-72: Advanced Marketing Tactics

These advanced marketing tactics get into the psyche of the customer and turns your Kindle eBooks into irresistible products. Some of these advanced marketing tactics require money and research while others are simple to implement but bring forth a dynamic change in your sales.

Method #67: Have A Teleseminar At Least Once Every Quarter

Having a teleseminar every quarter will allow you to connect with your customers and answer their questions on the spot. By answering people's questions on the spot, these people will be very grateful that you took their call and did a good job at answering the question. Since they are grateful for taking a few minutes out of your day to answer your question, these people will be more likely to buy your Kindle eBooks.

While you may not get a lot of people on the line during your first teleseminar, the amount of people you get on the line will gradually grow as you build a stronger presence for yourself on the web. Imagine what would happen if you got 1,000 people on the line and answered 20 questions. If you promote your Kindle eBook effectively during the teleseminar, you could easily be looking at 50 sales (assuming that 5% of the people who listened to your teleseminar will buy a $2.99 Kindle eBook is a very fair prediction to make).

How To Effectively Promote Your Kindle eBook During A Teleseminar

You need to promote your Kindle eBook at the beginning and end of your teleseminar. At the start of all of my YouTube videos, I mention a Kindle eBook that I wrote. After you mention the Kindle eBook, you need to tell all of the people on the line what you will be discussing today and when people can start asking questions. After you get all of the questions and discuss everything you said you would talk about, spend the last five minutes of your teleseminar talking about your Kindle eBook. The people who stayed on the line for the entire teleseminar may be very likely to buy one of your Kindle eBooks.

Better Yet, Have A Monthly Teleseminar
Having a monthly teleseminar requires more time, but if you were able to get 1,000 people on the line for all of those teleseminars, you would be able to boost your sales dramatically. If you had a monthly teleseminar for each of your Kindle eBooks, you would be able to have all of your Kindle eBooks land on the Top 100 Bestsellers Page for all of their categories. What's even better is that the people who listen to most of your teleseminars are going to be the ones who are very likely to be returning customers who buy all of the Kindle eBooks that you publish.
In addition to having a monthly teleseminar, you can record your past teleseminar and share that same one with your audience every week. You can send the same teleseminar to the people who did not see it yet.

Method #68: Give One Of Your Physical Books Away For Free In Exchange For The Customer's Email Address

Although this method is by no means free, it is a powerful way to get more sales. If you choose to implement this method, you need to make sure that it is still possible for you to make a profit. Brendon Burchard gives away a free copy of his book, *The Charge* in exchange for your email address (you still have to pay shipping). The people who get the free book get notified about Burchard's training courses and membership sites. Anyone who buys access to a training course or membership site allows Burchard to make a profit.

Charge For The Shipping

You do not want to lose too much money by implementing this tactic. In order to save a lot of money in the long run, you need to charge for the shipping. You still may lose $5 to $10 each time someone enters their email address to get your free book, but if that person likes your first book, then that person will be very likely to buy your other books as well. You can think of this as paid advertising, but this time, you will actually get a potential client's contact information as opposed to someone just reading your ad and clicking on the link.

This Method Has The Potential To Add Hundreds Of Extra Reviews To Your Book

If you give away enough free copies of your book, you will be able to get hundreds of extra reviews for your books. By having all of these extra reviews, your book will look more credible in the Amazon market place, and as a result, more people will buy your book directly from Amazon. In addition, by implementing Method #49, you will be able to give your other books more attention as well. Remember that most of your sales are going to come from Amazon, so you are going to make a profit from your book whether you have a training course up or just have your book. Buying copies of your own book for your customers will help bring it closer to Top 100 Bestsellers Lists in different categories.

Almost Guarantee A Good Review By Signing The Book

What takes less than a minute for you to do will be greatly appreciated by your customers. Not only does signing your book almost guarantee that the customer will leave a good review, but it will also give you a nice ego boost. Signing the book also gives your customer an ego boost. They get to show off your signature to your friends. Showing off your signature is another way of that person saying that they were good enough to get a book signed by you. As people show the book off to more of their friends, you will be able to boost your sales. Although you will have to perform small changes and do a small amount of work for your marketing strategy, for the most part, the book will market itself.

Method #69: Know The Customer's Psychology

One factor that plays a big role towards getting more sales is the customer's psychology. When you create a description or video for your product, you need that description or video to be optimized based on your customer's psychology. No matter what you are selling, whether you are selling a Kindle eBook about business or a training course about soccer, you need to understand the customer's psychology. This is how customers think and eventually decide if any product is worth buying.

1. **What do you do**? Customers buy Kindle eBooks written by credible authors that match their interests and niches. Not everyone will fall into this category which is why everyone (all 6 billion or so people on the planet) is not your target audience. You need to make it clear to the customer what you do so they know whether your Kindle eBook is the right one for them or not. Make your message clear

2. **Why should the potential customer care**? After you get through the first part of the psychological process, you need to make the potential customer care about what you do. If a potential customer does not care about what you do, then you are not going to make the sale. If you just told everyone that you are a social media expert, you would make people care by telling them how revolutionary social media has been for businesses and how some people get thousands of daily visitors to their blogs from social media alone. Don't assume that the potential customer cares just because they went to your product's link.

3. **How can the potential customer believe in you**? This is where you need to have a lot of credibility. It is easier to trust a social media expert with 100,000 followers than it is to trust a social media expert with 10,000 followers. Being an international public speaker, being a world-renowned person in your niche, and being the best in your niche are some of the many accomplishments that will make a potential customer more likely to believe in you. The most important way to get potential customers to believe in you is by having good reviews for your Kindle eBook. Almost every potential customer looks at the number of stars a Kindle eBook has or reads individual reviews before buying one of your Kindle eBooks. In other words, most of your potential customers will do their research before buying your Kindle eBook. By including testimonials for your Kindle eBooks, you will be satisfying this part of the customer's psychology.

4. **How can the potential customer begin**? So many people forget this step. After the first three parts get optimized, authors forget to tell their customers to buy their Kindle eBook. At the end of the description, you can say something like, "If you like the Kindle eBook, then use the free previewer to look inside the Kindle eBook so you know if this is the right Kindle eBook for you." Some of your potential customers will not take action unless you give them an action to take.

By understanding and mastering the entire psychological mindset of the customer and organizing it in the exact order it was presented, you may get a higher conversion rate for your sales. Getting more traffic is an important part of the strategy, but what happens once you get the traffic. Just because Amazon sends an email blast containing someone's Kindle eBook does not mean that Kindle eBook is going to make extra sales. Just because someone's blog is getting 100,000 visitors every month does not mean that person will get more sales than the person who is getting

100,000 visitors every year. It's great to have visitors, but it's just as important to have a high conversion rate. Appealing to a potential customer's psychology is a very powerful method to boost your conversion rate.

Method #70: Get At Least 10 People To Promote Your Kindle eBook Right From The Start

The more people there are who promote your Kindle eBook, the more likely your Kindle eBook will be to get more sales. As you self-publish more Kindle eBooks and build your presence, you will turn some of your customers into your fans who are eager to learn about your next Kindle eBook. They would also be very eager to help spread the word about your Kindle eBook. There are three kinds of people who would promote your Kindle eBook right from the start:

1. **Your fans**. These people will tell their friends about your Kindle eBook. However, those friends have to do research and then do the final search to confirm that your Kindle eBook is the right one for them. These people will help contribute towards getting more long-term sales.

2. **People you write about who submitted HARO pitches to your query**. These are going to be the people who show off your Kindle eBook to their friends with pride. Many of those friends will either buy your Kindle eBook or borrow it from someone because their friend got mentioned in the Kindle eBook.

3. **People who you give a special free prize to**. As you grow your presence, some people will think you are the best author around. These people would love to meet you in person and would do almost anything to promote your Kindle eBook. You can use your social networks to build a team of 10 non-paid promoters of your Kindle eBook. These people should be following you on one of your social networks or be friends with

you on another social network, and these people should be the ones who can do a good job at promoting your Kindle eBook. Then, you throw in the special free prizes. Everyone on your team gets a free, signed copy of your Kindle eBook when it comes out. If your Kindle eBook gets 5,000 sales within a certain amount of time (either 1 week or 1 month), then everyone gets free access to one of your training courses or free physical copies of some of your books. If the Kindle version of your physical book is priced at $2.99, getting 5,000 sales would result in you making $10,000 in one week or month. Giving away a free training course to 10 people wouldn't be so bad. Then, if you get 10,000 sales in the same amount of time ($20,000 for you), you can treat everyone to a nice dinner. You can offer more rewards such as a weekend vacation as your earnings from that one Kindle eBook increases. It will cost a good amount of money to pay for 10 people's dinners, but if you make $20,000 from it, then you will still bring in a big profit. In addition, the people who promoted your Kindle eBook will be able to meet you in person for the first time. That is the kind of experience that turns these people into returning customers who will tell all of their friends about you. As you do this more often, more people will rush in to promote your Kindle eBook and be on your team. When you get more people, some of those people will have large following and be more dedicated than others to promoting your Kindle eBook and watching it soar.

By getting at least 10 people to promote your Kindle eBook right from the start, you may end up making 20 sales in the first week assuming that all of these people have 1 friend who would buy your Kindle eBook right away. Making 20 sales in 1 week is enough to make the Top 100 bestsellers list for some of the categories your Kindle eBook is listed in. Then, Amazon will promote your Kindle eBook in its search engines, and the sales will continue to come in.

Method #71: Create A Free Sales Army

No matter how much effort you put into marketing your Kindle eBook, you and Amazon together will not be enough to turn your Kindle eBook into a bestseller. Instead of relying on those two things, you need to create a free sales army of people who will promote your Kindle eBook and get their friends to buy it. Some of your promoters will help you make more money. You may be wondering at this point how you can create your own free sales army. Surprising enough, creating your own free sales army is not as hard as it sounds.

The Easiest Way To Create A Free Sales Army

The easiest way to create a free sales army is by using HARO to gather sources. The more sources you include in your Kindle eBook, the larger your free sales army becomes. If you include 10 people in your Kindle eBook, those 10 people and some of their friends will become a part of your free sales army when they show themselves off to other people (by telling those people about your Kindle eBook in the process).

More Ways To Grow Your Free Sales Army

Although using HARO to gather sources is a great way to grow your free sales army, it is also important to grow your free sales army before your Kindle eBook gets published. Most of the people who you get as HARO sources to join your free sales army will only promote the Kindle eBook they get featured in. While this is a great start, it is important to keep people on your free sales army for your future Kindle eBooks as well. There are a plethora of ways to grow your free sales army so more people are buying your Kindle eBooks and telling their friends about them right when they get launched:

1. **Build your presence on your social networks**. Not everyone who follows you on your social networks will become a part of your free sales army. It is important to realize that social media is only a way to build awareness for yourself and your Kindle eBooks. Social networks do not result in a bigger free sales army. Instead, social networks result in more traffic to the page on the web that does grow your free sales army.

2. **Get more email subscribers**. The content you put on your social networks should point towards the content on your blog. After reading some of the content, your visitors will enjoy what they see. Some of these visitors will enjoy their content so much that they will enter their email and subscribe to your blog. Then, these people get notified every time you come out with a new blog post.

3. **Create a sales newsletter and build the list**. Getting people to subscribe to your blog is a very powerful and easy way to build your presence on the web. As these people continue getting and reading your blog posts via email, these people will trust you more. It is at this stage of the game when you will easily be able to tell people about your sales newsletter and get people to subscribe to that. If someone gave you their email address once, chances are they will give you their email address again.

4. **Your free sales army will grow itself**. If you master the first three tactics of growing your free sales army, it will simply grow itself as time passes. Friends will ask for advice, and then people in your free sales army will tell those friends about you. Then, those friends tell some of their friends and then the process continues on.

Method #72: Allow People To Vote On Your Next Kindle eBook

If you have four Kindle eBook ideas, and you don't know which one to write about first, leave it up to your customers. Have a poll in one of your blog posts with your four Kindle eBook options and ask your customers which Kindle eBook they want you to write. When you give your customers the option to choose which Kindle eBook you write about, you need to make sure you can write about all of the topics you chose. Giving your customers the ability to make you choose what your next Kindle eBook is about gives them power. The satisfaction of receiving this power will make these customers more likely to buy your Kindle eBook.

You Already Know Which Kindle eBook Your Customers Want

The Kindle eBook that received the most votes is the one that your customers want the most. This particular Kindle eBook idea is one that solves the problem that most of your customers have, and by writing this Kindle eBook, you will be able to get returning customers just by telling everyone that you wrote the Kindle eBook. By using more polls to get people's feedback, you will identify the problems that a lot of people have, and the best way to solve the problem is by writing a Kindle eBook on it.

Summarizing Methods 67-72

These powerful methods contain clever ways that you can get more sales for your Kindle eBooks. The more of these methods you implement, the more you will stand out in your niche. What other self-published author do you know of who does a teleseminar every quarter? Is that person also allowing his readers to vote on his next Kindle eBook? Imagine what would happen if you were able to implement all of these methods.

Methods 73-77: More Kindle eBook Marketing Tips

Last but certainly not least are five final methods that serve as the final touches that will allow you to boost your Kindle eBook sales. While some of these changes are quick to implement, others get implemented gradually over a longer period of time.

Method #73: Promote Some Of Your Kindle eBooks At The End Of Your Other Kindle eBooks The Right Way

Leaving links to your Kindle eBooks at the end of all of your Kindle eBooks is a great way to boost your sales for your existing titles. Most self-published authors who implement this tactic simply leave a giant list of their Kindle eBooks for the readers at the end of a Kindle eBook. Some of these lists go on for several pages. Instead of giving your customers an entire list of all of your Kindle eBooks on the last page of every Kindle eBook you write, only include the Kindle eBooks that are very similar to the one that the customer bought. Explain how all of these Kindle eBooks work together like a puzzle that ultimately gives the reader more knowledge or more fiction Kindle eBooks to read. Some of your readers will want to connect the puzzle right away, and the only way to do that is by buying more of your Kindle eBooks. As you repeat the process in your other Kindle eBooks, people will eventually solve the puzzle. Right when these people think they solved the puzzle, write another Kindle eBook and add it to the puzzle. If your puzzle never ends, and you continue to use your Kindle eBooks to promote each other, some readers will buy all of your Kindle eBooks.

Include Descriptions For Your Kindle eBooks

When you promote one of your Kindle eBooks inside another one of your Kindle eBooks, you need to provide a very short description that explains what your Kindle eBook is about. In this case, the ideal description is 2-3 sentences that very quickly summarize your Kindle eBook. If you want to increase your likelihood of getting the sale, include hyperlinks in your Kindle eBook that lead to the Amazon sales pages of your other Kindle eBooks.

Method #74: Remind People That They Do Not Need To Own A Kindle To Read Your Kindle eBooks

One of the main reasons why people do not buy Kindle eBooks is because they think that a Kindle device is needed in order to buy and read Kindle eBooks. However, this is simply not the case. There are several options people have to read Kindle eBooks without having a Kindle:

1. Use the Cloud Reader for PC and Mac.
2. Install the Kindle App in the App Store.
3. Install the Kindle App in the Android Store.
4. Install the Kindle App on your Blackberry.

The people who want to buy your Kindle eBook will be able to implement at least one of these four tactics to read Kindle eBooks without owning a Kindle. Most of your potential customers who do not have a Kindle will not buy your Kindle eBook just because they think there is no way to get it done. By mentioning these four options, your potential customers will realize that they can buy your Kindle eBooks without spending an extra $80 to buy a Kindle.

On your sales page, it is very important to include this information. You do not want to write a sales page that is over 2,000 words long only to realize that people did not buy your Kindle eBooks because they do not own Kindles. Including this information on your sales page, promotional blog post, and any other method you use to spread the word about your Kindle eBook will allow people to realize that they can buy your Kindle eBook.

When you teach someone a new skill (in this case, being able to read Kindle eBooks without owning a Kindle), that person may be more likely to buy your Kindle eBook.

By telling people that they can read your Kindle eBooks on an iPhone, an Android, and other devices, you are removing barriers that prevent people from buying your Kindle eBooks. With the exception of telling potential customers what type of person your Kindle eBook is for, you want to remove as many barriers that prevent people from buying your Kindle eBooks as possible.

Method #75: Word of Mouth

Word of mouth is a well-known way to get more sales. However, not every Kindle eBook is being shared through this marketing tactic. Not every self-published authors knows how to write Kindle eBooks that people talk about (and spread). In order to get people to spread your Kindle eBook through word of mouth, it needs to contain something that people want to tell others about. Here are some of the things that will allow your Kindle eBook to spread via word of mouth:

1. Best how-to content around
2. Best novel around
3. Eye-catching cover
4. Catchy title
5. Physical book
6. Your remarkable story.

These methods of getting more sales through word of mouth should sound familiar. They are topics that were previously discussed in this Kindle eBook. As people tell their friends about you, the amount of word of mouth sales you get has the potential to exponentially increase. As more people tell others about you, some people will buy your Kindle eBook just because your name is on the cover. There comes a point when someone hears many people saying good things about you, and then those people decide to buy one of your Kindle eBooks. If the customer likes your Kindle eBook, then that person may eventually buy your other Kindle eBooks as well.

Method #76: Create Infographics That Promote Your Kindle eBook

Infographics have become very popular on the web. Part of Mashable's success is because of its infographics, and it has been proven that social media posts with infographics get shared more often than social media posts without infographics. One of the reasons why infographics are popular is because they are easy to read and contain pictures. The cool design of infographics encourages many people to read the entire infographic. The best part is that most infographics take less than 15 seconds to read.

To quickly sum up infographics, they are really popular, and most people read the entire infographic. That means if you created an infographic for your Kindle eBook, most people would read the entire infographic. If you use enough cool pictures and have a cool design for your infographic, it will convince your potential customers to buy your Kindle eBook.

Hire Someone On Fiverr To Create The Infographic For You

Visual.ly is an option that many people recommend to create your own infographic. However, my advice would be to have someone create the infographic for you. You can get a good infographic designed on Fiverr for $5. Earlier in this book, I recommended using Fiverr to get a good cover design for your Kindle eBook. You can also use Fiverr to get a good infographic design at an affordable price.

When Is The Right Time To Take Infographics Seriously?
Just because you publish your Kindle eBook does not mean you should start implementing infographics to get more sales. In order to get more sales because of your infographics, you need to get people to read those infographics in the first place. Wait until you build a strong presence on your blog and your social networks before you create the infographic. The infographic is primarily a way for you to get a lot of sales during your launch so Amazon's search engines start to kick in. The infographic will make your review page look really good and help out towards getting more sales in the short-term and long-term.

Method #77: Submit Your Free Kindle eBook To The Right Websites
Submitting your Kindle eBooks to the right websites is one of the most important ways to get more sales for your free promotion. Some of the people who used this strategy reportedly got one sale every 10 seconds at certain points of the free promotion. Submitting your free Kindle eBook to enough of these websites may add up to 10,000 extra free downloads that you wouldn't have gotten.

What The Right Websites Are And Why They Work
The right websites to submit your Kindle eBooks to are the ones that are constantly promoting free Kindle eBooks. The reason these websites work is that some of them get thousands of visitors every day. In addition, the people who visit these websites know that the Kindle eBooks being promoted on that website are free. That way, people see the title of your Kindle eBook without thinking of the price. Since you are charging nothing for your Kindle eBook, you are removing the researching and final search from the buying process. All it takes is for someone to know about your

Kindle eBook and then make the purchase. You may not be getting thousands of daily visitors, and some of the websites you submit to may not be getting thousands of daily visitors either. However, if you submitted your free Kindle eBook promotion to 20 websites that get 500 daily visitors, then those websites combined get 10,000 daily visitors that can learn about your Kindle eBook. In total, that is 50,000 visitors who will learn about your Kindle eBook. Not all of them will buy your Kindle eBook, but if you submit to enough websites, you are easily looking at thousands of free downloads every day.

How To Contact The People Behind These Websites The Right Way
When you contact the people behind these websites to ask them to promote your Kindle eBook, you need to keep the email short and sweet. You will get more websites to promote your Kindle eBook if you send them an email with the following parts in the order they are presented:
1. **An introduction**. The introduction can be something like this: "I just wanted to let you know that I have a free promotion coming up for my new Kindle eBook, (What the Kindle eBook is about)."
2. **Tell the person reading the email what your Kindle eBook is about in less than five words**. While it will be tempting for you to tell the person reading the email everything about your Kindle eBook, keep it to under five words. Getting the website to promote your Kindle eBook is more important than you telling one person what your entire Kindle eBook is about from beginning to end.
3. **When the free promotion takes place**. This is what the person reading your email cares needs to know so that person can schedule your Kindle eBook to appear on the website at that time.
4. **The title of your Kindle eBook**. Now that the person reading your email knows about your Kindle eBook, tell that person the title of your Kindle

eBook. The more attention your title grabs, the more likely the website will to promote your Kindle eBook.

5. **A direct link to the Kindle eBook**. The person reading your email has other emails to read and no time to search around for your Kindle eBook. Adding a link to your Kindle eBook right after you tell the person your Kindle eBook's title will make locating that Kindle eBook on Amazon's gigantic marketplace much easier.

6. **The number of reviews your Kindle eBook got with the average number of stars**. The more positive reviews your Kindle eBook has, the more likely a website is to promote your Kindle eBook. These websites want to promote Kindle eBooks that provide their visitors with good content. If a website promotes a bad Kindle eBook, that lowers the website's reputation.

7. **Other places where you can be found on the web**. Include a link to your blog and your two best social networks. Too many links will overwhelm the person reading your email.

8. **A thank you as if the person reading the email already agreed to promote your Kindle eBook**. By the time the person reading the email gets to this stage, that person will be interested in promoting your Kindle eBook on the website. This almost seals the deal.

9. **Your signature.**The signature you leave behind reminds the person reading the email that you are a human too. That is one of the most important things to do that many people forget. It brings sincerity into the work you are doing, and in numerous cases, the signature seals the deal.

These are the 9 parts that when implemented in the order they were presented will result in more websites agreeing to promote your free Kindle eBook.

Two More Components That Get Websites To Accept Your Kindle eBook

Although the email you send has a big impact on whether the website promotes your Kindle eBook or not, there are two more components that are important towards getting the website owner to agree to promote your Kindle eBook. Just because you wrote a Kindle eBook and sent a well written email does not mean a website is going to take your Kindle eBook and put it up for thousands of people to see. These websites get numerous Kindle eBook submissions which means they have to say no to some Kindle eBooks. However, there are two things you need to follow to get websites to approve your Kindle eBooks:

1. **Quality content**. It seems like the importance of quality content couldn't be emphasized more than it already has in blog posts and Kindle eBooks like this one. However, it is an important factor that decides whether the website owner accepts your request or not. Unless your Kindle eBook is *really* bad, then websites will show your Kindle eBook to their audiences. Most websites judge your Kindle eBook's quality based on your Kindle eBook's reviews. The more reviews you have, the better. If you can't get reviews on your own right now, get friends to review the Kindle eBook for you. After your Kindle eBook gets promoted on multiple websites, you will easily get more reviews.

2. **Give the people behind the websites enough time to read the email you send them**. If you ask the website owner to promote your free promotion that is going on right now, then its too late. In order for most website owners to say yes to your request, you need to tell them about your free promotion's dates one month in advance. That gives you enough time to contact a lot of website owners while getting more of them to say yes and promote your Kindle eBook.

Once you master sending emails to website owners, you will get more of them agreeing to promote your Kindle eBook each time. In addition, the entire process of submitting your Kindle eBook to website owners is a universal rubric. That means you can send the same exact email to multiple websites. Once you get the email down right, there's no need to create another custom email. Just use the rubric you have so you are able to save more time and submit your Kindle eBook to more websites.

How Many Websites Should You Submit Your Kindle eBook To?
The more websites you are able to submit your Kindle eBook to, the more sales you may be able to make. You should submit to at least 10 websites, but if you have a rubric email in place, you should submit to as many websites as you possibly can. If you can submit your Kindle eBook to 50 websites, then you will get a lot of exposure for your Kindle eBook. If you are able to submit your Kindle eBook to 100 websites, then that's even better.

76+ Websites To Submit Your Kindle eBook To
Shelley Hitz wrote a great blog posts which sums up this method and provides over 76 different places where you can submit your Kindle eBooks. Just Google, "76+ Places To Submit Your Free KDP Select Promotion for your Kindle eBook" and her blog post is the first one that comes up.

Summarizing Methods 73-77
Implementing these methods are the icing on the cake. These methods will allow you to see a boost in your sales, but some of these methods such as Method #77 cannot be implemented right away. You may have to hire someone to make your infographic for Method #76, but having an infographic is not necessarily the make or break point of your Kindle eBook. An infographic is merely something nice to have for your Kindle

eBook. It's a great way to stand out in your niche, but one infographic is not going to be responsible for a majority of your Kindle eBook's sales. You should only implement Method #76 when you are making a full-time income from your Kindle eBooks. The other methods should be implemented as soon as possible.

I Need Your Help!

I am very appreciative that you chose my Kindle eBook over a whole bunch of other options on Kindle marketing. Thank you for getting my Kindle eBook and reading all the way through. My mission as an author is to provide content that works and allows people to get better results. That is why I would appreciate a quick review for this Kindle eBook.

I would love to know which method resonates the most with you and which three methods you will implement immediately. Keep me posted on your progress.

About The Author

Marc Guberti is a teenager author, speaker, and social media expert who teaches aspiring entrepreneurs at Fordham University every summer about creating their own thriving businesses. Marc has one of the most popular social media blogs in the world which can be found at www.marcguberti.com. Marc also offers Twitter Domination and Power Blogging training courses which you can see at www.udemy.com/u/marcguberti. Stay connected with his future works by following him on his social networks and by subscribing to his blog.

More Of The Author's Books

This book is one of the parts to a giant puzzle that has the potential to turn your self-publishing into a full-time income.

How To Publish More Kindle eBooks Faster shows you exactly how you can write more words and do just what the title says: publish more Kindle eBooks faster. Publishing more Kindle eBooks faster will mathematically make your dream of making $100,000 every year by self-publishing Kindle eBooks easier to attain.

Keep The Ball Rolling gives you the motivation you need to finish writing your eBooks. Too many people stop writing their eBooks not because they chose a bad topic or because they can't write about the topic but because they lack the motivation and desire to continue writing the eBook. *Keep The Ball Rolling* shows you how you can stay motivated throughout your self-publishing career.

How To Be Successful On Twitter goes into great detail on how you can thrive on Twitter. Imagine what would happen if you got more engagement and targeted followers on your Twitter account. You would be able to get more blog traffic, more Kindle eBook sales, and more credibility on the web. *How To Be Successful On Twitter* will show you how to thrive on a powerful social network and spread your content 140 characters at a time.